I0092528

INDIE AUTHOR CONFIDENTIAL 8

SECRETS NO ONE WILL TELL YOU ABOUT WRITING

M.L. RONN

Copyright 2022 © M.L. Ronn. All rights reserved.

Published by Author Level Up LLC.

Version 2.0

Cover Design by Pixelstudio.

Cover Art by jasoshulwathon.

Editing by BZ Hercules.

Time Period Covered in This Book: Q1 2022

Special thank you to the following people on Patreon who supported this book: Zhade Barnet, Stephen Frans, Michael Guishard, Jon Howard, Beth Jackson, Mojo Jojo, Lynda Washington, and Etta Welk.

Some links in this book contain affiliate links. If you purchase books and services through these links, I receive a small commission at no cost to you. You are under no obligation to use these links, but thank you if you do!

For more helpful writing tips and advice, subscribe to the Author Level Up YouTube channel: www.youtube.com/authorlevelup.

For avoidance of doubt, Author reserves the rights, and no one has the rights to reproduce and/or otherwise use this work in any manner for purposes of training artificial intelligence technologies to generate text, including without limitation, technologies that are capable of generating works in the same style or genre as the work without the Author's specific and express permission to do so. Nor does any person or company have the right to sublicense others to reproduce and/or otherwise use this work in any manner for purposes of training artificial intelligence technologies to generate text without Author's specific and express permission.

CONTENTS

ABOUT THIS SERIES

This isn't your typical writing self-help book. This series is a compilation of lessons learned from an indie author trying to walk the path to success. Follow author M.L. Ronn (Michael La Ronn) as he navigates what it means to master the craft of writing, marketing, and running a profitable publishing business. Learn from his successes and failures, and learn about things that most successful authors only talk about behind the scenes.

To read all the collected volumes of this series in an anthology, visit www.authorlevelup.com/confidential.

INTRODUCTION

I always love starting a new year. The first quarter is always a power quarter for me. I often get more done in the first quarter than other quarters combined. There's something about the winter that inspires me to work faster. It's probably my go-to combination of tea and moody jazz, which is always a more effective combo when it's cold and depressing outside. They help me think deeper. Winter is often my most intellectually creative season for this reason.

2022 promises to be just as crazy of a year as 2020 and 2021. There's still so much uncertainty about the COVID-19 pandemic and how it is going to end, but there are some positive signs that the virus is weakening. Hopefully, that's true for all of our sakes. This disease is driving people nuts, literally and figuratively.

2022 also represents a clean slate for my writing business because I've streamlined my strategy to three strategic pillars instead of five. As a result, I have fewer goals to achieve, which gives me more clarity and focus as I target the most important tactical objectives.

My Core Strategic Priorities

As a refresher, my mission is to create content that entertains and/or educates my audience, preferably both, and to remain nimble in an ever-changing industry. I do this by focusing on three strategic priorities:

- Become a world-class content creator
- Become a technology and data-driven writer
- Become the writer of the future (looking forward)

I believe these three priorities are most important for me to have a long-term, sustainable career.

I have updated the format of this book moving forward. There will only be three sections—one for each strategic pillar—and you can expect approximately 10 chapters in each (down from 12).

By streamlining future volumes of *Indie Author Confidential*, I will free up more time to write fiction, which has always been my focus. But you can still expect the same quality of content in this series.

What's in This Volume

This volume is the most diverse volume I have written yet.

In the World-Class Content Creator section, I discuss lessons learned from getting COVID a second time, an important lesson I learned from studying Dean Koontz this quarter, and a new approach I took to managing my intellectual property that is already paying off massive dividends. I also talk about my exploration into creating my first large print edition.

In the Technology and Data-Driven Writer section, I discuss why I finally made the leap to purchase 1000 ISBNs.

This was a big deal for me, and it opens up so many capabilities that I didn't have before. I also talk about experiments with AI-assisted software for writing my books and why it's a cornerstone of my production process moving forward. I also discuss a colossal success in Q3 2021 that turned out to be a colossal failure. Funny how things change in just six months.

In the Looking Forward (formerly Become the Writer of the Future) section, I talk about the dizzying number of technologies that will be coming in the near future, how I dealt with a recent bout of overwhelm, the continued rise of cover design costs, and what I would do if I were starting my writing business again today in 2022. I am calling this section Looking Forward because I will use it to discuss the future of writing, but also other topics that don't neatly fit into the other categories.

Like I said, I cover a lot of ground in this volume, and I hope it makes for intriguing reading.

Enjoy this volume.

M.L. Ronn
February 1, 2022
Des Moines, Iowa

BECOME A WORLD-CLASS CONTENT CREATOR

DEALING WITH COVID (AGAIN)

In January 2022, I tested positive for COVID-19. I'm fairly certain it was the Omicron strain.

At the time, I was fully vaccinated and boosted. I had cold-like symptoms and a sore throat for several days. Fortunately, I was fine with no long-lasting symptoms or long COVID.

The illness took me away from writing for a week because my entire family caught it.

My then manuscript-in-progress went untouched. My emails piled up. I had to postpone a speaking event. I missed a week of work.

Yet, something miraculous happened.

My books kept selling.

I landed a speaking engagement.

My business bills remained paid.

When I recovered and sat down at my computer to write, I picked up where I left off. After two days, I was caught up.

Having COVID helped me slow down and reflect on what is most important. It also helped me think about the future of my writing business. That was a blessing.

In the grand scheme of my lifetime, one week is nothing.

The week after COVID, I wrote 20,000 words, which more than made up for the week I lost. The law of averages is always in my favor.

Don't beat yourself up if you have to take time away from your writing. It'll all work out in the end. What matters most is that you sit back down and resume when you're recovered.

A REMINDER THAT TABLES OF
CONTENTS ARE UNDERRATED

While researching for my book, *The Author Estate Handbook*, I wanted to find some good resources.

I was browsing for legal books on the topic. Wills. Trusts. Estate planning basics. Executor guides. I had a lot of choices.

The experience was a powerful reminder of how important tables of contents are for nonfiction. Out of the 12 or so books I browsed, one of them had an amazingly granular table of contents. It was much more detailed than the other books, whose contents had an air of sameness about them. It didn't just have a chapter on wills—it had several subchapters, each one exploring a different legal problem with wills. It did this for every chapter.

After reading the table of contents, I felt like the book had so much more to offer, even though it was the same length and in the same price range as the other books. I bought it without hesitation.

It was a reminder to me that tables of contents are prime real estate in my nonfiction books. If you can show value in the table of contents by being more thorough than comparable books, you'll stand out.

I took that lesson to heart again when I wrote *The Author Estate Handbook.*

DEAN KOONTZ PATTERN INTERRUPTS

I was reading *Odd Thomas* by Dean Koontz. I had a bad experience with Dean Koontz in the early 2000s—I read *Watchers* and didn't like it. I thought I wasn't a Dean Koontz fan until I read *Odd Thomas*. Now he's one of my favorites. Funny how one book can distort your perception. It's easy to forget that authors evolve, and that one book isn't truly representative of an author's aesthetic.

As I was reading the book, section after section captivated me. I wondered how Koontz did it.

After I finished reading, I went back to a few of the sections that I enjoyed and tried to dissect them to see if there was anything I could learn.

To say that I learned a lot was an understatement. Studying Koontz was like walking through the doorway to another world.

I could talk about many techniques that Koontz uses that I will soon be incorporating into my own work, but the one that resonated with me most was his pattern interrupts.

I wrote a book called *The Writing Craft Playbook*, and it is a recap of a few techniques that mega-bestsellers use to keep readers hooked. In that book, I talk about the concept of fiction as fabric. Let me explain this before I dig into Koontz's technique.

A few years ago, my wife and I visited an outlet mall. This outlet mall has stores by many designer brand names. You can often buy clothes at this outlet mall for much cheaper than you could, say, on the coasts.

But there is just one problem with this mall: sometimes the clothes have defects. I once bought a shirt where the seams were crooked. I've learned to be careful when shopping here, so I inspect my clothes thoroughly before I buy them.

During this shopping trip, I happened to buy some dress shirts, and I specifically remember checking the seams due to my last bad experience.

After buying my shirts, I followed my wife around one of the women's clothing stores. Normally, on a trip like this, I like to find a couch or a bench and write on my phone or read a novel while my wife shops. This outlet mall doesn't have anywhere to sit—I'm convinced it's by design to get people to shop or leave.

Anyway, I had to stand around while my wife shopped, and I happened to be reading *Jurassic Park* by Michael Crichton at the time.

As I was reading, I noticed that Crichton writes in 400-to-500-word sections, followed by a "turn of thought," which is a sentence that transitions the story. For example, he'll write 400 words from the perspective of the viewpoint character about a scientific concept, and then the phone will ring, launching them into a conversation. The phone ringing is the turn of thought. The turn of thought acts as the "seam" that holds the two pieces together.

If you read Crichton's work, it's just a patchwork of little sections. The turns of thought happen like clockwork. Once you see this, you can't unsee it. It's true of almost all the mega-best-sellers.

This is where Koontz comes in. He helped me take the concept further. If you break a 400-word section into two pieces, there's another divider: a pattern interrupt.

A pattern interrupt is a change in focus. It guides the reader's eye, much like a cut in a television show or a movie. That's the best way to think about it.

Here's what I observed in one of Koontz's chapters:

- It begins with approximately 100 words of setting.
- A pattern interrupt shifts the narrative focus to the character taking an action (walking down the street). This is just one sentence.
- The narrative returns to the setting, capping it with a photographic turn of thought (the character looking up at the stars).
- Whereas the turn of thought is at the story level, the pattern interrupt is at the narrative level. The author uses them to switch cleanly between different narrative styles like setting, character voice, action, and dialogue.

This was an "a-ha" moment for me because what it really means is that a novel is just a series of 100–200-word sections. You can write 100-200 words in a few minutes. Write them, ensure that they're appropriate, finish nicely with a pattern interrupt, and every other pattern interrupt, use a turn of thought.

It's so simple! But man, simple ain't easy.

To reiterate that, here's what it looks like on the page:

- 100-200 words of a narrative choice (action, dialogue, setting, character voice, and so on)
- Pattern interrupt that uses another narrative element
- 100-200 words of a narrative choice (perhaps the same as you started with)
- Turn of thought that finishes the section cleanly
- Repeat

I know this makes fiction sound formulaic, but that's not what I'm suggesting. If you did this over and over in your novels, then it probably wouldn't turn out well.

I am suggesting that if you look at the works of mega-bestsellers, you'll see this pattern. It's one of many variations they use. You may even be doing this yourself and don't realize it.

It's an unconscious thing. I don't think authors do it on purpose. But it's perhaps the closest thing I can find to perfect form.

That's an important lesson that Dean Koontz taught me.

QR CODES IN A PAPERBACK

A reader emailed me with some questions. One of them was what I thought about putting QR codes in a paperback that take readers to a certain place.

I've heard of this over the years, but I never really considered it. QR codes are mainstream, but they never really took off the way people thought they would. Android users are familiar with them because QR codes are built into the Android operating system, but Apple dislikes them. They make you take a bunch of steps to scan a code.

That said, I still think it's a great idea. It got me thinking about what a proper execution would look like if I ever wanted to do it.

You can create QR codes on many websites for free with an account. You can route people to a website link or a document. It just takes a few seconds.

Let's take the following use case: in one of my paperbacks, I want to include a QR code that routes people to my next book. I could send them to the book's sales page on my website, or I could route them to a service like Books2Read where they can choose where to purchase the book right away.

I only have a few concerns. What if QR scanners become obsolete? That would be a problem.

That's why I keep coming back to just using a simple link. As much as I like the idea, I think QR codes are more work than necessary. I do like the idea, and using them lends a certain professionalism to your marketing, but it's more to manage and maintain.

OVERVIEW OF MY MASTER
PUBLISHING FILE

Last quarter, I wrote a book called *Keep Your Books Selling: How to Manage Your Book Portfolio and Make More Money.* The book gathered the lessons I learned while cleaning up my book files and sales pages.

I learned that running an organized, logical publishing business is more difficult than it seems. I also learned that no matter how organized I am, none of it will matter if I don't leave written documentation.

I began the process by asking, "What do I need to know about my books?"

I remembered reading a book by M.L. Buchman called *Planning Your Author Estate.* In that book, he gave away a free "master publishing file" template that helped you gather all the metadata for your books. It's an ingenious tool. I used that as a foundation. Many hours later, I had my own master publishing file, and boy, is it powerful.

I'll quickly cover what I capture on the spreadsheet.

- Series and series number
- Title, subtitle, and any previous titles

- Author name
- Year written
- Book type (novel, writing book, short story collection, and so on)
- Genre and subgenre
- Publisher
- Publishing style (traditional or indie-published)
- Word count
- Print page count
- Book formats published (e-book, trade paperback, audio, and so on)
- ISBNs
- Unique store identifiers (such as ASINs)
- Price per format
- Original publication date
- Date copyright registered
- Copyright registration number
- Links for the major retailers
- Distributors that carry the book (like Draft2Digital and PublishDrive)
- Book Funnel link
- Cover designer and year designed
- Cover design cost
- Whether I have font and image licenses on file for the cover
- Whether I have model releases on file for the cover
- Whether I have the cover source files and draft materials on file
- Prior designer information
- Current version published
- The date that version was uploaded
- The date the book passed EPUB validation

- The date I checked all internal and external links in the book
- File formats I have saved the book in
- Book description version and date published
- Editor information and dates edited
- Editing cost
- Whether I have the edits on file
- Trade paperback trim size, interior color, and page color
- Hardcover trim size, interior color, and page color
- Audiobook publication date, narrator, and ACX contract terms
- Whether I have the audiobook MP3s on file

That's not all of the fields, but it's most of them. I did this exercise for every single book I published. To say it was tedious and painstaking is an understatement.

But this process helped me create a system that I can replicate for every new book that I publish. A few days after I publish a book, I simply fill out the spreadsheet. All the data is captured once and forever.

Even better, I can use the master publishing file to run pivot tables. Earlier this quarter, I decided that I wanted to jump into hardcovers all-in. I've dabbled with them, but now I'm ready to run. However, KDP Print and IngramSpark have minimum and maximum page counts for hardcover books. I needed to know quickly which of my books fell outside the boundaries. In just a few seconds, I created a pivot table that gave me a list of books that I could not publish in hardcover. Everything else was eligible.

This exercise also helped me spot gaps in my catalog. For example, I discovered that I had accidentally left the price of one of my books at $0.99! I also realized that my pricing strategies needed some work. I was able to see the prices of all my books in one place, and that helped me determine a better strategy.

The exercise also prompted me to review my pricing strategy in international currencies. I wasn't always consistent with how I priced a book in England, for example. Now all of that is fixed.

I also discovered, to my embarrassment, that I had published a Book 1 in a series with a 6x9 trim, but the sequels were 5.25 x 8. Oops!

These things happen, especially if you don't have a system. Fortunately, they can all be fixed. This exercise helped me clean up my portfolio, make more money, and increase the value of my portfolio overall. I believe having a well-managed portfolio of intellectual property is important, especially when you have as many books as I do.

I'm so glad I took the time to do this project. It took a lot of time, effort, and money, but it has already paid for itself. I have more peace of mind than I ever had in my early years of publishing when I only had a few books. I'm never more than a few clicks away from knowing what's going on with all my books. That's something every author should strive for.

THE AUTHOR HEIR HANDBOOK: AN INTELLECTUAL SWING AND MISS?

This quarter, I finished a book called *The Author Heir Handbook*, which is a follow-up to *The Author Estate Handbook*. It's the heir's guide to understanding and managing a literary estate. My master plan with the book was to recommend it at the back of *The Author Estate Handbook* as a must-buy for authors to give to their heirs. I envisioned it as a perfect stocking stuffer or something to slip into a safe deposit box for an heir to read when an author passes away.

I thought it would be a good idea to write a book for author heirs because, to my knowledge, there are no books on the market for them. Trust me when I say they are going to need a lot of help. I predict there will be a cottage industry of free-lancers who exclusively work with author estates in ten to twenty years once many prominent self-published authors start dying.

I like to establish thought leadership for opportunities like this. I tend to be ahead of my time when it comes to these types of books, but the investment will pay for itself in the long term.

I decided to write the book and jumped in without thinking too much more about it. As I wrote the book, something didn't feel right. I didn't like the "tone" of the book. It felt like I was just giving orders, and I didn't think that's appropriate given the fact that many heirs' situations will be different. With authors, I feel more comfortable doing that because, well, I'm an author!

I scrapped the book. I *never* do that. I commit to a book, write it with every inch of my soul, publish it, and then forget about it. But I took a few days to rethink this book because something about it bothered me.

What I realized (and should have known) was that this book is technically for a different target audience. It's not for authors; it's for heirs. And, if my hunch about heirs is correct, they won't have any understanding of the publishing industry. I couldn't use jargon; I'd have to use plain English. I would have to explain the writing life in ways that I haven't explained it before, and I would have to do it for an audience whose background would be far more diverse than my typical author audience. An heir could be twenty years old or seventy; they could live in any country in the world; they could be tech-savvy or barely use a computer; and most importantly, they could all be inheriting vastly different estates. An heir whose author followed my *Author Estate Handbook* would be in a much better position to manage the estate than an author who did no estate planning at all.

I'll admit that this realization disoriented me. If I was going to approach the book again, I'd have to do it with a softer touch and a different angle.

I tried again.

Here's how I did it.

First, I committed to plain English. I don't know if I succeeded, but I tried. I really did. In retrospect, I think writing a calculus book would have been much easier than trying to explain the publishing industry to non-publishing people.

Second, I kept the paragraphs short. I hit the Return key more than I usually do. I kept the sentences short too. And most importantly, I capped almost all the chapters at around 1500 words, which I think is a nice bite-sized length. Many were less than that. Smaller chapters are easier to consume.

Third, I defined all terms. I never assumed that the heir knew what a term meant. Much of the book is defining terms and explaining them with simple examples.

Fourth, I took the approach of giving the heir awareness rather than explaining in detail *how* to do something. I used the chapters to explain a problem, give examples of how one *might* solve the problem, and then mention the names of sites or resources the heir can look up to find more information. This is a double-edged sword because some readers will definitely want more hand-holding. But as I pointed out, this is impossible to do that because every reader is starting from a different place. I had to keep the book high-level, which goes against my nature given that *The Author Estate Handbook* was the most detailed book I've ever written. There was no way around this.

Fifth, I had to omit some topics. I completely stayed away from any legal or financial topics, again because I didn't know where the reader would be coming from.

The result was a 30,000-word nonfiction book that I hope will give heirs a foundation of what they need to know about running an author estate. It walks them through securing the estate, organizing the estate, and managing the estate. I teach them how to create an inventory of the author's books (using a streamlined version of a master publishing file), how to update books on retailers, and how to refresh books over time with new covers, new book descriptions, and more. There's also a chapter on marketing.

Will the book be successful? I have no idea. It was the most difficult book I've written since *The Indie Author Bestiary*.

Do I care if the book is successful? Not really. I committed to the idea, saw it through, and now it's in the world.

There are only three possible futures for a book:

- it will perform poorly, selling a few copies every now and again (but still increasing my income over time)
- it will sell as well as my other titles
- it will outperform everything and change the trajectory of my writing business as I know it

You never know what will happen until you publish. *The Author Heir Handbook* was an interesting intellectual challenge, and it taught me some valuable lessons that I will apply to future books.

LESSONS FROM CREATING MY FIRST LARGE PRINT EDITION

I finally broke down and bought ISBNs. That's a huge deal for me because I've been so resistant to doing it in the past. I'll talk about that later.

But now that I have ISBNs, I can create additional formats for my books. One of the first items on my list is large print editions.

This was especially on my mind as I created *The Author Estate Handbook*. The content lends itself to a large print edition.

I spent a weekend educating myself on the format and how to create it.

The target audience for large print editions is seniors and the visually impaired. Therefore, large print editions must follow certain rules to be considered large print. Some publishers only publish large print editions, which I found fascinating.

I'll recap what I learned about creating this format and the steps I took to successfully create my first edition.

. . .

Formatting Considerations

First, I had heard that Vellum can create large print editions. I create all of my other editions in it, so I figured I'd try it. While Vellum can create large print editions, it misses some key elements of the format. I found myself shaking my head as I created my large print edition in Vellum.

Atticus handles large print editions much better. It's still not my main formatting app yet because I believe it still needs some work, but in the future, I may consider moving my large print editions to it.

Large print editions will always have more pages than a trade paperback because the font size is bigger. The recommended font size is 18 points with 1.25 or 1.5 line spacing. The margins in a large print book are wider too. All of this will increase your printing costs considerably, so indie authors should use the biggest trim size they can to keep the costs down. That size is 6.14 x 9.21, but you could also do 6 x 9.

It is also recommended that the body font in a large print edition be a sans serif font to increase readability. (Vellum only offers serif fonts—one of the reasons why I shook my head.)

You cannot have smaller fonts in the book than your body. This means that if you have images with captions, you have to remove the captions and make them part of the body text. You also must put footnotes at the end of a chapter and make them big enough to read.

You should use block paragraphs instead of indentations, and the text should be left-justified (ragged right). Hyphenation at the end of a line is a big no-no.

You should also avoid large blocks of capital letters, particularly in chapter headings. Unfortunately, this is something I cannot avoid at this time.

Images should be aligned to the left to improve readability, which is something Atticus can do (but Vellum cannot).

Another important element of large print editions is to avoid italics. I'm guilty of using italics a lot in my nonfiction. I'll be rectifying that moving forward. It is recommended that you replace italicized text with bold text instead.

Cream pages are the best recommendation to help with contrast. Fortunately, all my books are in cream anyway.

So, if I look at the requirements for a large print edition, I can meet all of them except:

- sans serif font
- no large blocks of capital letters in the chapter headings

Complaints about Vellum aside, that's not bad. It's not perfect, but it's not enough to hold back creating an edition. I believe that the Vellum developers will eventually get this right, and when they do, I can regenerate titles and reupload them as needed.

Marketing Considerations

It's critical to differentiate a large print edition from the regular trade paperback. Otherwise, you'll have some disappointed readers.

For this reason, it's a good idea to include the words "Large Print Edition" in the book title when you publish it. KDP Print and IngramSpark also let you designate a title as a large print edition.

You should also put a button on the cover with the words

"large print" on them. This will make it easy for readers to see that it's a special edition.

I would also recommend putting the words "large print" on the title and copyright pages of the book just to cover all of your bases. This way, no one can give you a bad review claiming they didn't know what they were buying. If they do, it's clear that they can't read.

Make sure you don't forget the back cover. It should also be in a sans serif font in a big font. I suspect many people are missing this one.

You've also got to think about a pricing strategy. If your trade paperback is priced at $14.99, you might want to price the large print at $16.99 or $18.99, depending on the printing economics. Whatever you do, you should have a strategy so your large print pricing is uniform across titles.

(Oh, and I forgot to mention that you can create hardcover large print editions too! Libraries prefer large prints hardcovers because they last longer.)

The main goal is to get the large print edition to show up next to the trade paperback on the striker's sales page. This makes the book look more professional.

In researching this, I noticed that a lot of authors weren't doing this. In fact, the large print edition was the only edition of the print book on the sales page. I believe the reason for this is that there is a data issue between Amazon and Ingram, and it's easier for authors to create a large print edition as the only edition.

From what I could tell, the proper way to handle this is to create all your paperbacks on Ingram and don't use KDP Print. Otherwise, Amazon may suppress the Ingram versions. I don't know any of this for sure; these are just observations. But in my opinion, it doesn't make sense to only have a large print edition as the paperback unless your target audience is seniors or the visually impaired.

There's another key issue that I believe is preventing more authors from creating large print editions: retailers don't really like them. Amazon is biased against them. You have no idea if a book is a large print edition until you click on it. It shows up as "paperback" on the sales page. You have to click into additional formats to see the large print edition, but even then, you won't see it unless the author put the words large print in the title. You'd think Amazon would be better about this.

So, the burden is on the author to let readers know large prints exist. You could do this by putting a line at the top of the book description that says "Now available in e-book, paperback, audio, and large print!"

You should also consider putting this on your website, with a direct link to the large print edition. Otherwise, readers won't know that it exists.

As I said, there's a lot to consider, and a lot of steps to follow if you want to do this correctly. I observed several self-published authors on Amazon who are not publishing large print editions correctly, and I think that's going to come back to bite all of us if retailers ever decide to start enforcing rules.

I believe we are in the early days of self-published large print editions. At some point, retailers will make it easier to publish them and easier for readers to find them.

My strategy moving forward is to publish large print editions on day one. It's just a few extra steps for me in the publication process, and the design cost is minimal.

The real question is how I plan to handle my backlist. At some point, I would like to enable large print editions for my backlist, but that will require a considerable time and money investment that may not provide a profitable return for a long time. I'll probably create large print editions for a few titles per year and whenever I refresh covers.

MAXIMIZING MY PORTFOLIO

In a previous chapter, I talked about creating my master publishing file. It allows me to know what's going on with my books.

It also helps me spot opportunities and fill in gaps. A question I've started asking is "What can I do this month to maximize my portfolio?"

What if I could wave a magic wand and make my portfolio the best it could be? What would that look like?

For starters, I would have:

- All of my books available in e-book, trade paperback, hardcover (dust jacket), audiobook, AI audiobook, and large print editions.
- All of my books at all possible retailers and distributors that are willing to carry them, with bookstores and libraries able to buy any book in my catalog.

I can do all of this now, whereas I couldn't necessarily do it a few months ago before I purchased ISBNs.

Since I have fewer goals for 2022, I've decided to spend a few hours each month maximizing the portfolio. In reviewing the first quarter, I identified the following opportunities with just my 2014 titles alone:

- I can create an audiobook edition of my book, *Muse Poems*. The audiobook would be less than an hour and cheap to produce. While I probably wouldn't make much from this edition, it would fill in a gap.
- Remove an early audiobook from sale. I did this on a royalty-share on ACX. I need to pull the book down because it no longer fits in my portfolio. This will require me to buy out the narrator on ACX.
- Create a new cover for my short story collection *Reconciled People*. It's the oldest cover in the portfolio and it desperately needs a refresh.
- Expand my distribution to StreetLib, which is a European book distributor that distributes to many retailers around the globe that I can't reach with my current distribution partners.
- Republish all my paperbacks with a new ISBN and distribute them on IngramSpark. This will make them available for bookstores and libraries.

Which one should I do? There's no wrong answer. I'll probably do several of them this year, prioritizing the ones that will bring me the most income first.

Tending to a book portfolio is like tending to a garden. There's always something to do, and if you want a nice garden, you have to spend more time than anyone else is willing to spend.

I'm excited about this new way of thinking about my books,

and I know that it is going to pay dividends over the next decade.

CORRECTING A MISTAKE FROM THE PAST

The first year of any author's publishing career is probably riddled with mistakes. I am no exception. I made almost every mistake you can imagine in 2014.

I was learning how to write fiction and dealing with all the struggles that go along with being new to the craft.

I was learning book formatting, and while my e-books looked okay, my paperbacks looked awful.

I spent a fortune to buy a trademark, which I ended up abandoning because I quickly realized my mistake.

I spent money on marketing in all the wrong places.

My early covers were awful.

And that's just scratching the surface. Perhaps one of my biggest mistakes in 2014 was engaging in royalty-shares with audiobook narrators. It sounded like such a great idea at the time—pay nothing upfront, get a great-sounding audiobook, and then share royalties with a narrator!

Except that the royalty-share is in perpetuity. There is no time limit on it. Almost all the early titles I produced did not sell a single copy. As a result, I can't do anything with the format. I can't pull it down and create a new edition because I signed a perpetual contract. Again, colossal mistake. If I knew what I know now, I wouldn't have done it.

That said, the narrators I worked with were fantastic people and they all did a great job.

I reviewed the ACX contract and determined that there is a way out of the royalty-share agreement: buying out the narrator. I have heard of authors doing this.

I decided to see if I could reduce the number of royalty-share titles in my catalog to maximize the number of rights I have. One of those was for my book *Eaten: The Complete First Season*, which I ultimately rebranded, rewrote, and republished as *Food City*. The audiobook is just floating out there. It hasn't sold a single copy since 2015.

I offered to pay the narrator a generous sum that accounted for what I would have paid them plus what the title could have earned over the next seven years. The narrator accepted the offer, we signed a contract that I drafted, and we contacted Audible to have the title removed. Once they did, I paid the narrator and rested easy knowing that I could pull the title down and not have any encumbrances on it moving forward.

I take full responsibility for the title. It was unfair to the narrator to create a title that didn't do well, and I view it as my responsibility to do something about it. This was an expensive mistake but one that I'm thankful I can correct. Over the next few years, I'll work with my narrators to dissolve royalty-share agreements that didn't turn out the way we both hoped. But I have to do this while ACX allows it, and while the narrators are still alive. Otherwise, if a narrator passes away, I am literally stuck in a perpetual agreement, and I have no idea if the narrator has heirs who will even receive their share of the income. My only option at that point will be to use copyright termination, and I'm not so sure that it would work because I would still own the copyright—I would have just given away perpetual distribution rights.

Yep, this is what happens when you don't think ahead. But as I said, most mistakes in this new world of publishing are fixable. At least I didn't give away the copyright or lose the rights to the work, or worse, all my works. It's just a constant reminder that there are always consequences to everything you do.

HOSPITALITY WOES

I traveled recently and stayed at a hotel. My wife and I like this particular hotel franchise because it is family-friendly. We have stayed at this hotel many times, but this was the first time we stayed there since the pandemic began.

The hotel had completely changed.

The lobby was dirty.

The two front desk attendants carried on a long conversation as if we weren't standing there waiting to check in.

The room was barely clean and didn't feel fresh.

The breakfast and happy hour were pathetic, with old food, watered-down beer, poorly mixed drinks, and employees who seemed to hate their lives.

And don't even get me started on the swimming pool—I'm convinced the water was carrying legionella. I did *not* swim in the pool.

I couldn't believe how far the hotel had fallen. It wasn't just one thing—the entire experience was bad. Even my seven-year-old daughter kept complaining, and she's normally a chipper kid who sees the best in every situation.

The pandemic hadn't been kind to the hotel. I learned that

they suffered from staffing shortages because they laid off much of their staff during the early days of the pandemic and couldn't find anyone to replace the original staff when the economy came back. They were also struggling to keep their occupancy rates high, which meant they had to drop the room rates...which explains why our stay was so cheap.

If that's not a death spiral, I don't know what is. I don't expect the hotel to remain under the current owners for long. They have two to three years max, and that's being generous. I felt bad for the establishment.

Later that month, I needed to schedule my car for routine maintenance at my local dealership. I generally reserve curse words for auto dealers, but I like my current dealer a lot. They were very fair with me when I bought my first car, and they have a package where you can get an oil change, tire rotation, and a car wash for very cheap. The technicians have always been honest with me. They've never put pressure on me to make a repair or pulled any funny business that dealers are notorious for. And trust me, I've dealt with a lot of crooked mechanics.

This dealer's service was impeccable. They had a shuttle service that I used whenever I had to drop my car off during a weekday. I got to know the shuttle drivers, who were great guys. In the early days of the pandemic, the shuttle drivers would come to my house to pick up my car so I could stay home. They did it for no charge.

And then, something happened. I usually schedule my appointments online, but I noticed that the website calendar wasn't working. I sent the dealer an email letting them know that the site was broken. I didn't receive a reply.

A few days later, I tried again with no luck. This time, I used the online chat feature—the representative didn't even bother to help me.

I called the dealer and told them about the issue on their website. I left a message. My voice mail went unreturned.

I called again and had to schedule an appointment over the phone with an employee who had terrible phone skills. I told them about the website issue and she said they'd look into it.

Three months later, they're just now getting around to fixing it...I can't imagine how much business they lost during that time. I'm a patient guy. I bet the average person would have just called someone else.

My appointment didn't go well. The technician seemed rushed, and he overcharged me. When I caught the billing error, he promptly corrected it, but the damage had been done. It was clear that I needed to find another shop.

I learned that the dealer was acquired during the pandemic by another, larger dealer conglomerate from out of state. This conglomerate, clearly incompetent, didn't like how the dealership was run, and when they tried to implement new cost-cutting rules, the staff walked out. This explained everything. I bet the dealer is hemorrhaging customers.

My point in telling you both of these stories is that the pandemic has wreaked havoc everywhere. The institutions we know are no longer the same.

The hotel I had fond memories of is now just a memory. The dealer I could trust can no longer be trusted. Now I have to find new service providers in many areas of my life. It is requiring a lot of time and effort.

Excellent customer service is almost impossible to come by right now. I can't think of the last time I had a pleasant experience calling a company since the pandemic began. People are stressed out and they have realized that their employers don't care about them. Many employers acted shamefully during the pandemic, and they got away with it.

At an employer like that, why should employees care? Especially at a call center, which was probably hell on Earth *before* the pandemic? I don't blame the employees for feeling or performing the way they do, though it is inconvenient for me. I especially don't blame them for quitting and leaving a staffing shortage.

Out of this vacuum will come opportunities. Companies who treat their people well *and* who manage to maintain superior services and products despite the devastation of the pandemic will do very well.

Some hotels found ways to weather the pandemic, and those are the ones that will survive. Same with auto dealers. But, in all cases, I would bet that they were well run before 2020.

That got me thinking about authors. The pandemic has hurt the publishing industry, authors included.

Has the pandemic blunted your customer service? Are there parts of your platform that need to be refreshed, such as parts of your website, contact forms, or other reader-facing items? This is a good time to check all your touch points with readers.

The last thing you want readers thinking right now is that you don't care.

Readers, like me, are experiencing terrible customer service everywhere too. Don't add to it. If you can strive to be a positive example, then you'll be fine.

My customer service commitment has always been to respond to emails quickly. While my response times did get slightly longer during the worst early days of the pandemic, I still respond to emails very quickly.

I keep my website up-to-date and my contact form operational. I added direct sales functionality in 2020. I'm exploring cryptocurrency functionality now. I'm always looking for ways to remain relevant and provide great service to my fans.

I keep publishing books at a regular pace. I keep trying to help people whenever I can. I hope that my stock is growing during the pandemic. I know that many authors have slowed down during these times, maybe even stopped writing altogether.

But here I am, and I plan to keep going, business as usual. Several years from now, I believe that is going to make a big difference.

BECOME A TECHNOLOGY
AND DATA-DRIVEN WRITER

WHY I FINALLY TOOK THE LEAP ON ISBNS

I finally bought my own ISBNs. After spending $1500, I am the (not-so-proud) owner of 1000 ISBNs.

I bought the block of 1000 because I have 74 books at the time of this writing, and my plan is for all my books to be available in e-book, trade paperback, hardcover, audiobook, and large print. That's at least 370 ISBNs that are spoken for. That leaves 630. If I publish books in five formats moving forward, this block will last me for 126 books. It took me about 10 years to write 100 books, so if I keep my same pace, I estimate that this block of ISBNs will last me at least that long.

The *only* reason I bought them was that I had a windfall of income near the end of 2021 and I need to make a big expense to defray the tax consequences. Seriously. That's the only reason I bought them.

Will this block of ISBNs earn me more than $1500? I think so. It will allow me to open up to new sales channels that I haven't been in before, like bookstores and libraries.

The next questions I had after buying the ISBNs were:

- How do I clean up the mess I've made for the last eight years by *not* having them?
- Do I need to republish my books to use a new ISBN?

I definitely created a mess, and there's no way around it. When you publish an e-book, you have one opportunity to enter an ISBN. If you don't, the retailer assigns a free one for you. The only exception is Amazon, which only uses ISBNs for documentation purposes. You can update an ISBN there after you publish a book.

You also lock in a free ISBN when you publish a paperback title. The only way to undo this is to unpublish the paperback and republish it with a new ISBN.

Therefore, I've decided that the best course of action is to update my ISBNs whenever I refresh titles. For example, I'll be republishing my *Good Necromancer* series with new covers and interiors sometime in 2022. I'll also be putting them under my Michael La Ronn pen name. Since I'll have to unpublish the titles anyway, I'll just use new ISBNs at that time.

At some point, I'm also going to refresh my short story collection *Reconciled People*. While I don't need to unpublish it, I'll probably do so just so I can put a new ISBN on it.

Over time, as I refresh my books, they'll all eventually get new ISBNs. This way, I'm only doing a few titles at a time and it will minimize disruption.

When you publish a new book, you have to update your website with new links, which makes this a pain. But there is definitely a benefit to having all official ISBNs on all titles in my catalog.

What if, one day, one of my books takes off and sells millions of copies? What if bookstores and libraries suddenly want more of my titles? They'll be able to buy them if I have official ISBNs. If my portfolio is a patchwork of official and unofficial ISBNs, it will hurt my professionalism.

So yes, that's the price I've paid for the last eight years. Was it worth it? Yes, I think so. I've said for a long time that I can use $1500 way more efficiently than purchasing ISBNs, and that has been true.

Now that I have this capability, I'll use it and see where it leads me.

SUDOWRITE

I've started experimenting with AI-assisted writing tools. The one I like and have been using is Sudowrite.

Sudowrite is built on the GPT-3 AI engine. It reads the text you've written and then recommends a block of 100 to 200 words as a jumping-off point.

When you have written at least 200 or so words, you can use a feature called "The Wormhole," which generates text for you. You have several options to choose from. You can import the suggested text exactly as-is, modify it, or not use it at all.

Sudowrite doesn't write your story for you, but it offers alternative directions you can take the text that you didn't consider. Sometimes the suggestions make no sense, but more often than not, they're interesting and cogent. I find this feature endlessly fascinating.

I don't think AI-assisted writing tools will replace writers anytime soon. But I do think they should be part of your author toolbox.

Another way I've been using Sudowrite is with dictation. I use it in Chrome for Windows along with the Dragon extension so I can dictate my words directly into the browser. After about

30 seconds of dictating, I hit the wormhole and see where it takes me.

I haven't used Sudowrite to write full books yet. So far, I've just been experimenting with it here and there—not enough to put a disclaimer in my books.

In Q2, I will incorporate Sudowrite into a new fiction series to see what happens. I'll click the wormhole every 500 words or so. I'm curious to see what would happen if I did this for an entire novel, or even an entire series.

If you use a tool like this that much, then I believe you should disclaim it on the copyright page so you're transparent with readers. The tool does generate text for you, so, in a way, it's a shortcut.

There are also problems with these tools, though. First, you have to be careful that you don't lose your author voice. Just because a tool recommends text, it's still not smart enough to identify what makes you YOU.

Also, these tools are often used out-of-context. If you don't use them consistently, it doesn't know what came before and it won't know what comes after. This is still a major problem with artificial intelligence and natural language processing. You're using it to generate text for the moment, which is problematic when you're telling a long-form story.

I actually think these are good things. It keeps you in control of your stories.

Oh, and by the way, I wrote this chapter with Sudowrite (but you probably knew I was going to say that). This chapter is approximately 600 words, and Sudowrite generated around 200 of those words.

If you extrapolate this throughout a novel, then it's possible that for a 50,000-word novel, then Sudowrite would generate around 16,500 words, or 33 percent.

Would this enable you to write fiction faster? Or would you

have to spend more time in revision? It's a fascinating question that I look forward to answering in the next volume of *Indie Author Confidential.*

LESSONS IN TWO-FACTOR AUTHENTICATION

While on my estate-planning journey, I learned a lot about two-factor authentication (2FA). 2FA has been around for a few years, but it's still not widely adopted. The average person has no clue how it works or why it can be detrimental to your heirs if you pass away suddenly without a plan.

I thought I would share a chapter from *The Author Estate Handbook* that covers 2FA. You may find it useful.

———

At the time of this writing, two-factor authentication (also known as 2FA, two-step verification, multifactor authentication, or MFA) is a relatively new security feature that requires a user to enter a second proof of identification to access an account.

With traditional logins, you have to enter a username and password to access an account. With two-factor authentication, you have to enter your username and password *and* verify that you are the owner using an additional method. Usually, that method is a one-time passcode that is sent via text message or email. The code is time-sensitive.

Many banks require 2FA as an additional security measure, but most companies do not require it. At the time of this writing, you usually have to opt-in for it.

I strongly recommend that you use 2FA to secure your accounts to give yourself added security while you're alive. It is designed to be foolproof, and with a few exceptions, it is. You may be using 2FA on some of your accounts already.

Another potential danger you should be aware of is identity theft after death. Cyber thieves troll obituaries and death records to look for easy prey. They can file tax returns under your name, open bank accounts, and wreak all sorts of havoc that your heirs will have to clean up. If you don't follow cyber best practices while you're alive, you will be defenseless after you're dead.

Consider that, as an author, you're a public figure, and if you've achieved some success, there may be some publicity about your death so that people can pay tribute to you. That's a prime opportunity for a thief to look for accounts to hack into— no one's going to be paying attention because they'll be busy grieving, after all. 2FA keeps you protected.

However, if you do use 2FA in any capacity, be very careful. If not, your heirs will be locked out of your accounts even if they have your usernames and passwords.

That's why 2FA is a Silver Bullet of Doom. You may be required to use it already on some sites, and more sites may require it in the future. You will not be able to get around this problem.

Most people right now are using their phones for 2FA, which is dangerous in several non-obvious ways. I bet you have received those text message passcodes again and again and never once thought about how screwed your heirs could be if they don't have access to your phone. If something happens to your phone while you're alive, you'll be locked out of your accounts until you can buy a replacement. If you die and your heirs disconnect your phone without understanding 2FA, they'll be locked out of your accounts forever.

At this juncture, you have a critical question to answer: are you using 2FA today in any capacity?

If the answer is no, the next critical question is whether you should. If you choose not to, fine.

If the answer is yes, then you may have an existential threat to both your personal and author estates. You must read this chapter and you must make sure you understand it. 2FA is not difficult, but some people may find it a little too technical and "techy." I won't deny that.

If 2FA doesn't make sense after reading this chapter, I recorded two short videos so you can see it in action. I'll link to them at the end of this chapter.

Please note that failure to take steps to address the 2FA problem may doom your author legacy. If I sound overly alarmist, it's because I don't believe enough authors understand how much danger 2FA is to their estates. I predict that too many people are going to learn the hard way. This chapter will open your eyes to just how problematic 2FA can be, and how you can address the problem safely.

Now that I've rung the alarm bells enough, let's turn them off and talk about the different types of two-factor authentication methods.

TEXT MESSAGE (SMS) AUTHENTICATION

. . .

With text message authentication, the company sends you a text message with a one-time passcode that you must enter after inputting your password. This is also known as SMS authentication. To validate your account, you must have your phone nearby. Your phone serves as your key.

SMS 2FA is the most common verification method, but it is the least secure because of an attack hackers can use called "SIM swapping." In a SIM swap attack, a hacker calls your cell phone provider and pretends to be you. They convince your provider to switch your phone number to a different SIM card. Then, when they log in to your accounts with your username and password, they receive the one-time passcode to their phone.

The chances of a SIM swapping attack are rare for most people, but it could happen.

There's another better reason not to use your phone for two-factor authentication that I mentioned previously: if something happens to your phone, you won't be able to receive text messages until you find a replacement. When you die, your phone number will eventually be terminated. What happens, for instance, if you die and your heirs disconnect your phone without realizing that they need it to authenticate your accounts? Uh oh.

Even if your heirs keep your phone active for a time, they're going to have to cancel it at some point. That's why SMS authentication is a bad idea. Yet, at the time of this writing, many companies *only* offer SMS authentication, which makes the issue more difficult. Cyber security professionals have been urging companies to move away from SMS authentication for the reasons I mentioned in this section, but companies are reluctant to do so.

. . .

MOBILE PROMPT AUTHENTICATION

Some companies such as Google rely on an app that already exists on your phone to authenticate your account.

For example, at the time of this writing, Google will ask you to open a Google app on your phone such as YouTube. When you do, a code will appear in the YouTube app and you have to match that to the code in the account where you are trying to log in.

These types of prompts are tied to your phone number. As with SMS authentication, if your phone is lost, you can't authenticate, which will lock your heirs out of your accounts.

EMAIL AUTHENTICATION

Instead of an SMS notification, you can elect to have your one-time passcode sent to your email address, which is much safer, but not 100 percent secure if your email accounts are ever breached.

However, email authentication is much better than SMS because if something happens to your phone, you can access your email from any device that has an internet connection. If you secure your email address with a strong password and two-factor authentication (for your email account itself), then it is a safe way to authenticate your accounts. Logging in to your email may be less convenient than receiving a text message, but it's still a good way to protect yourself.

Also, it's worth pointing out that if your heirs don't have access to your email accounts, then you're relegating them to doom because they'll never be able to pass 2FA for any other account you have.

APP AUTHENTICATION

You can also authenticate your account using a dedicated authenticator app. Examples include Google Authenticator, Authy, and Microsoft Authenticator. I use and recommend Authy.

All authenticator apps are free and they work the same way: they generate one-time passcodes for your accounts and change them every 30 seconds. You log in to your desired account with your username and password, open your authenticator app, grab the code, and you're in.

At first glance, authenticator apps usually scare people off because they look way too complicated, but they're not. They're not immediately intuitive, though.

To set up any authenticator app, the steps are the same:

- Go to your account dashboard, enable two-factor authentication, and then select the authenticator app option. You will see a QR code appear on the screen.
- Open your authenticator app, select "Add Account," and that will activate your QR scanner. Scan the code.
- In your authenticator app, you will then be given a one-time passcode that expires in 30 seconds. Enter the code in your desired account to complete the authentication.

- The next time you log in and are asked for the code, open your authenticator app to get it.

The major benefit of authenticator apps is that they can be used on *both* desktop and mobile devices. This means that if you pick the right one, you won't be married to your phone for codes.

Some password managers such as 1Password also allow you to generate one-time passcodes within the app. You'll see it next to your password. However convenient this is, this is less secure, because if someone hacks your password manager, they can get your codes too. It's probably safer to use a separate authenticator app.

The authenticator app I recommend is Authy. Authy works on both your desktop and phone, and it allows you to sync your account between devices. This means that if anything were to happen to your phone, you can still get the one-time passcode on a computer. Your codes are stored in the cloud, which could be a concern for some, but they are encrypted on your computer before they're sent to the cloud, so you have pretty good security.

Security experts don't recommend using cloud backups for 2FA, but the small tradeoff in security is worth it for one important reason: your heirs can install Authy on their computer, link your account, and start getting the codes right away. It's very, very useful, and it will get heirs around this Silver Bullet of Doom.

I recommend an authenticator app as your primary or secondary 2FA method.

PHYSICAL SECURITY KEY AUTHENTICATION

. . .

If you want the best security of all, you can buy a physical USB security key. After you enter your username and password, you insert your security key into a USB port on your computer or the charging port on your phone. Some sensors require you to tap the key or scan your fingerprint to authenticate your account.

This is a YubiKey 5C NFC. You insert this into a USB-C slot and then tap the gold button on the key to authenticate. It fits easily on a necklace or a key ring too.

Physical security keys are considered to be the safest authentication method because hackers can't fool them. They also can't replicate them digitally. A hacker would have to hack your accounts *and* steal your security key, which is next to impossible.

There's another good reason to use a security key. Sometimes, hackers can use a trick called "spoofing." With a spoofing attack, the hackers create fake websites that look eerily similar to the real ones, such as a bank's website. They lure you to the website by sending you an email or text pretending to be the company you trust. If you enter your credentials, they'll steal your login info. A security key can detect spoofs because it scans the website domain. It will only work on the real version of the website, therefore frustrating hackers and alerting you to the fact that you were fooled. You can then immediately change your password and report the attack.

You can also take security keys with you everywhere you go. They're small enough to fit on a keychain, in a wallet, or on a necklace.

I recommend the YubiKey brand. There are many models to suit your needs, but most IT and cybersecurity professionals agree that these are the best security keys on the market. Another prominent security key model is Google Titan.

On a desktop or laptop, you can leave your security key in a USB port so that you don't have to insert it every time you need to authenticate your accounts. As long as the key is in the port, you'll enjoy near-automatic authentication.

On a phone, security keys are a little more cumbersome, but not very. You will have to insert the security key into your charging port every time authentication is needed. However, some keys support near-field communication (the same technology that powers Apple Pay and Google Pay), and you can tap the key on the back of the phone to authenticate, which is much more convenient.

I paid around $50 for each of my security keys. New models are coming out all the time, so research the one that is best for you.

If you buy a security key, buy at least two: one as your primary, and another as a backup that you keep in a fire-resistant safe or safe deposit box. You can link both to your accounts. Most places that accept security keys allow you to link an unlimited number of keys to your account. This way, your heirs can use *any* of your keys.

Security keys aren't well-supported right now, but I expect that to change in the future.

BACKUP CODES

Some providers give you one-time backup codes to use in case you are locked out of your account. These are the option of last resort, but useful if you ever need them.

If a company gives you backup codes, store them in a safe place. Write them down or put them in a password-protected file. Don't be the person who doesn't write them down and then needs them someday!

SECURING TWO-FACTOR AUTHENTICATION FOR YOUR HEIRS

At the time of this writing, not every website supports 2FA. Not every site supports it equally either.

Most banks don't support authenticator apps or hardware keys yet, so you're forced to use SMS.

Some sites like Adobe only allow SMS and email authentication.

Other sites, like Google, Facebook, and Amazon allow for all authentication methods.

As a result, if you use 2FA, you're likely using a patchwork of different methods, which is the biggest drawback right now.

My 2FA strategy is to use physical security keys as my primary method wherever and whenever possible, and an authenticator app as my secondary method. If absolutely necessary, I will use email authentication. I disable SMS at any place that will let me. I'm betting on authenticator apps and security keys enjoying better support in the future. I may be wrong, but at least I know I'm taking the best steps to secure my accounts.

Your strategy could look like mine, or it could be more conservative, with you enabling as many 2FA methods as possible to maximize your heirs' chances of recovering your accounts. It's up to you.

It's not enough just to use 2FA while you're alive. You must also be thoughtful about how your heirs will get your passcodes.

WHERE TO START

It doesn't matter whether you like 2FA and use it regularly or if you actively avoid it. Chances are high that you're using it *somewhere*, and you need to document where. Otherwise, your heirs will be locked out of your accounts.

Use a site like the 2FA Directory to determine which sites support 2FA. Go through the list slowly and write down the websites where you have accounts. Don't rely solely on your memory; you may forget one or two websites and that could be troublesome for your heirs. Some password managers like 1Password can also alert you to which companies support 2FA.

Also, go through your favorite bookmarks to see if there are any additional sites where you use 2FA.

Create a password-protected spreadsheet that records how you're addressing 2FA. I've created a template for you at www.authorlevelup.com/2FAtemplate. Modify it as you see fit. I also have an Estate Plan Organizer Excel sheet that I'll share at the end of this book that also includes a tab for 2FA.

Next, go to each website and determine which 2FA methods they support, and which ones you are willing to use. Record the website and mark which methods you are using on the spreadsheet. If the service offers backup codes, create a separate tab on the worksheet and paste your codes there.

As an obvious reminder, you'll also need to update the spreadsheet any time you create a new account that supports 2FA.

Next, password-protect the spreadsheet and store the password both in your password manager and in your fire-resistant safe or safe deposit box.

Creating this spreadsheet will be a pain, but it's the best way of getting your heirs around the two-factor authentication problem that I can think of. Otherwise, you're forcing them to guess where you've used 2FA and you're increasing the chances that they won't be able to find your codes.

Also, consider imparting some strong words to your heirs: *Under no circumstances* should your phone line be disconnected until all 2FA websites have authentication disabled or have been updated with a new phone number that your heirs will have access to. Otherwise, they could be cutting themselves off from your accounts.

FINAL THOUGHTS

When used with a password manager, two-factor authentication will maximize your security with:
- secure passwords that are difficult for hackers to guess
- passcodes that hackers won't have access to

2FA isn't the most convenient thing in the world to use, but it's critical. Many experts say that you should enable it on your email accounts, bank accounts, and other sensitive financial or health accounts at a minimum. I recommend adding it to any account you have that provides it, especially your writing-related accounts.

Two-factor authentication is a must-have in today's digital world. Not every website supports it, and most that do allow it to be optional. As cyberattacks continue, more websites will change their stance. Try if you want, but you won't be able to get around this problem even if you actively avoid 2FA.

At the time of this writing, few writing-related websites even offer it. Amazon and Draft2Digital are the first that come to mind. Expect more retailers to offer it in the coming years, either as a result of a security breach or because of user demand.

If you still need help understanding how 2FA works, I've created two short videos to help you see it visually:

•Two-Factor Authentication Explained in Three Minutes
•How to Set Up an Authenticator App in Three Minutes

You can watch the videos at www.authorlevelup.com/2FAvideos.

If you're interested in *The Author Estate Handbook*, you can grab it at www.authorlevelup.com/estatehandbook.

AMAZON KDP PRINT WOES

I feel like I was the only person in the self-publishing space that had serious troubles with KDP Print last year.

Usually, I can rely on KDP Print to be my most trusted retailer channel when it comes to publishing and updating books. The paperback versions of my books are almost always available before the e-books. The same goes for any changes that I make to my books.

But in Q4 of 2021, KDP Print had major problems. A site-wide bug afflicted their servers, and it prevented changes from getting through.

I know this because it coincided with my book portfolio refresh that I covered in *Keep Your Books Selling*. Almost all of my 70+ books were updated in some form during this project.

I didn't have any problems until around book 50. Then, I noticed that the changes I requested weren't going through.

When I built my master publishing file, I implemented a versioning system on my book interiors. You can find them on the copyright page of any book I publish. You'll see "Version X.X." This helps me know which version of the book is for sale. I implemented a versioning system across all of my books exactly for the problem I'm about to describe. It's unobtrusive for the reader and helps me stay organized.

Most people would publish an update and not think about it ever again. But what happens if the retailer doesn't accept the update? You'll never know about it.

If you publish a book with some minor changes to the interior, how will you know if those changes were made? You could check the sample, but if the changes you made were past the sample, then you don't really know for sure.

That's why a versioning system helps. I keep a change log on my computer that describes the changes I made in each version of the book. Then I put the version number on the copyright page. After I upload the book, I set a calendar reminder to check the sales pages of the book across all retailers in 48 hours. If the sample on the retail page shows the correct version number, then I know the change went through. If it doesn't, then I know either to wait or to check for an error on the dashboard.

I was making changes to my paperback editions on KDP Print and the correct versions weren't showing up in the sample after a week. I emailed the KDP Print support team, and they informed me about the bug. They also assured me that the correct version would be printed if a reader purchased the book (but I don't know about that).

After the new year, I resubmitted the changes and everything appears to be fixed.

That's why you should develop a system for quality-checking your books. If you don't, then little things like this will slip past you. They'll add up over the years. The impacts could range from minor issues in the case of a few typos, or major issues in the case of broken links that should have been repaired, incorrect calls to action at the back of the book, or major plot holes that you fixed at the last minute and didn't want readers to see.

I am now organized enough that I know when a change doesn't make it through a retailer, and that's a beautiful thing. I'm in a much better place than I was a year ago.

THE THREE-MINUTE CHALLENGE

I went to my local UPS store where I have a mailbox. I stuck the key in the lock and it didn't work. I asked the store employee what happened and they asked who I was. I gave them my name, and they said I wasn't in their system.

They gave my mailbox to someone else and didn't even tell me!

I spoke to the manager and he apologized and promised to get to the bottom of it. He asked me to produce documentation for the mailbox.

I whipped out my phone and, within three minutes, I had a copy of the mailbox agreement, my most recent renewal, and a confirmation email from the store confirming that my registration was valid.

Thank God I am fairly organized. I had just restructured all my bookkeeping folders the week prior as part of a cleanup project (which I'll discuss later). I took a lot of time structuring that folder in particular so that expenses would be very easy to find. That little bit of foresight paid off big time.

Lo and behold, I got my box back, but imagine what a pain

in the ass it would have been if I had to spend hours looking for documentation (if any existed).

As I was in the store hammering out this problem, I came up with a little game that I am going to hold myself to moving forward.

The game is this: any time I am presented with the task of finding anything related to my writing business, I must find it in three minutes or less. If I do, I win. If not, then it's a failure and I have to rework things so that I can find it in the future quickly.

When I made it home, I did some "drills" to test how organized I was. I passed most of the time.

Let me give you four simple (but not necessarily easy) challenges and see if YOU can pass them.

If you can pass all these challenges, you are on the right track with your writing business. Remember, you have to be able to find the answer in three minutes or less.

- Challenge #1: Write all businesses expenses that you made on this day, two years ago. Bonus points if you can find the receipts for those expenses before time is up.
- Challenge #2: Generate a list of all services that you currently pay a subscription for your writing business (hint: domains, email marketing, and so on).
- Challenge #3: Write down the total amount of your business expenses for the current year. No "going from memory." It needs to be as exact as possible.
- Challenge #4: Write down how much money you made on all book retailers last year. If you're exclusive to Amazon, your challenge is to write down how much money you made per format (e-

books, paper, audio). No need to itemize this by
book—just the amounts.

Can you find the answers to the challenges above in three
minutes or less?

I can. Sure, I cherry-picked the examples, but the point
stands.

Here's why these challenges are important.

Challenge #1: Knowing your expenses is important. If you
have a service like QuickBooks, then you can nail this one.
Being able to find a single expense at any time, anywhere
quickly is critically important. What happens if you get audited
at tax time and receive a bunch of questions about a particular
expense? What if you have to settle a dispute, as I did with my
mailbox?

Challenge #2: If you got hit by a bus tomorrow and your
heirs needed to stop credit card payments for certain services,
where would they start? For example, if I die, I don't need Phot-
oshop anymore. That subscription needs to be canceled on day
one. Otherwise, my bank account will leak money that my heirs
could be enjoying.

Challenge #3: Again, you can nail this one if you use Quick-
Books or a similar service. Knowing your expenses is critical. It's
also critical for your heirs to know your expenses and income for
at least three years prior, as you can still be audited even when
you're dead.

Challenge #4: Knowing how much you make at each
retailer in a given month is soooo nice. It's not easy to do,
though. There are tools such as Scribecount that are making
sales tracking easier, but I don't believe in tying myself into a
paid ecosystem to glean data that I should already know. But a
service like this would be wonderful for heirs.

Think about it: every minute you spend trying to find something is a minute you can't spend writing. That adds up. Not to mention the stress from not being able to find something when you need it.

The next level of thinking here is, could your heirs pass these challenges in three minutes or less? If so, wow. Congratulations.

Every minute your heirs spend finding something is robbing them of their own passions and obligations too. Getting organized is really being kind to them after you're gone.

USING AI FOR AUDIOBOOK PROOFING

I recently spoke with a company called Pozotron, which aims to use artificial intelligence for an unlikely task: proofing audiobooks.

In a previous volume of this series, I wrote about the importance of audiobook proofing. I committed to hiring an audiobook proofer, as there is a cottage industry of people who provide this service now.

I never considered that AI can help with this.

The software works by scanning your text and comparing it to your audio. It marks any discrepancy between the two.

You (or an audiobook proofer) can review the discrepancies and approve or reject them. When you're done, you generate a list of timestamps that need to be corrected along with a summary of what needs to change. You give this to your narrator and they make the necessary corrections.

Authors can use audiobook proofing software to help them proof. It's slow-going, tedious work, and I think many authors would welcome the assistance.

Audiobook proofers can use this software to enhance the

value of the services they provide. It ensures they will catch even more errors.

I see it as a win-win and an elegant solution to an existing problem.

MY WRITING APP DATABASE: A LESSON IN FAILURE

In the previous volume of this series, I wrote about my book *The Writing App Handbook*.

I developed a database of writing apps to help writers find the perfect match.

I hired a developer who created a well-designed and easy-to-use database. I loved it, and early users in my community did too.

I committed to maintaining the database. When I priced it, I set aside a percentage of the development costs each year for maintenance because I knew that WordPress updates would facilitate maintenance.

What I failed to realize, however, was just how frequently I would have to update the database. I thought it would be a once-a-year occurrence. Boy, was I wrong!

I deployed the database in June 2021. In September, it was broken. Other than updating WordPress and plugins, I didn't make *any* updates to my website or do anything that would've broken the database. And trust me, I was very careful to avoid breaking the database.

My developer fixed the problem quickly and we got the database up and running again.

Then, in January, it broke again. At this point, I exceeded my maintenance budget. It wasn't worth it if I had to hire someone every 90 days to fix the database, especially since it is not monetized.

So I did the math and decided to retire the WordPress database. I'm not going to spend any more money on it. Did I hire the wrong developer? Maybe, but I like to think I vetted them pretty thoroughly.

I replaced the database with a Google Sheets spreadsheet. It's not nearly as elegant, but it still gets the job done.

This was a failure, and an expensive one given that I have nothing to show for it. But I did learn a lot about website development and just how expensive it can be.

URBAN FANTASY DATA AND ANALYTICS IN 2022

Every year, I purchase a K-Lytics Report on the status of the Urban Fantasy and Paranormal Romance market. Since it's my main fiction genre, I like to keep track of how the genre is evolving. I've bought the report every year since 2017. My, how the genre has changed, and my, how it has stayed the same.

Out of the top 300 titles, 66 percent of the books have female protagonists. This has been the case for as long as I can remember. About 10 percent of the books feature male protagonists, 8 percent feature a couple or team, and 12 percent feature a symbol.

I write primarily male protagonist urban fantasy. I'm still in the minority.

Google search interest in Google fantasy peaked in 2012 and reached its lowest point in 2017. Search interest is back to 2014ish levels, but it has been on somewhat of a downturn.

On average, there are approximately 40 to 60 new urban fantasy and paranormal romance titles released each month on Amazon. Most of those are in Kindle Unlimited.

Out of all analyzed books on Amazon, the most common price point was $4.99, which indicates that authors can get away with higher price points than the basic $2.99. This is useful to know because I have been pricing my Book 1s at $2.99.

Ninety-five percent of the top 20 sellers in urban fantasy and paranormal romance are in Kindle Unlimited, which is crazy. If you look at all books in the genre, around 60 percent are in Kindle Unlimited. I'm willing to bet that closer to 80 percent of those titles that are self-published are in Kindle Unlimited, but that's just a guess. Given that Kindle Unlimited is predominantly in the United States, this means that 60 percent of urban fantasy and paranormal romance cannot be found anywhere other than Amazon.

Short reads (books less than 100 pages) only account for 7 percent of sales.

The average book length is around 328 pages.

Those are just some of the key data points from the report.

I'm always careful not to put too much stock in a report that only captures data at one retailer. There are also some data problems inherent to Amazon, like the fact that categories don't actually match the content of a book. Authors abuse the category system and get away with murder. So, you don't really know how a true subgenre is performing without doing more digging. However, K-Lytics offers a useful starting point.

Some things that were very clear to me after reviewing the report:

- Male-driven urban fantasy represents a long-term opportunity. It's a smaller pool, which means I can make a name for myself in it.
- Male-driven urban fantasy represents a long-term opportunity for retailers outside of Amazon because all the bestsellers are in Kindle Unlimited.

- I need to write more titles with male protagonists until I have a hefty number. It will give my brand more staying power.
- I need to develop a marketing strategy for retailers outside of Amazon. No one will be doing this, so it will be a good idea to gain an advantage for myself.
- The genre seems on the verge of another breakout a la *Twilight*. Interest is rising again, and it's probably just a matter of time before we see another mega title.

Most importantly, this data is a reaffirmation to keep writing and to keep moving in the same direction. As a genre hopper, I used to say that I couldn't find a genre I could settle down in. I always struggle to find a niche. I think I've found one now, so I just need to keep at it.

MY INITIAL THOUGHTS ON CRYPTOCURRENCIES AND BLOCKCHAIN

I've been watching cryptocurrency and blockchain closely. I still haven't taken any action, but I'm fascinated by how the technology is evolving.

A few years ago, I would have put cryptocurrencies into a "hype" category. There are a lot of people pushing it who clearly just want to make money.

There are a lot of things I like about crypto and a lot of things I don't like.

Let's start with what I like.

I like the anonymity that crypto provides. Being able to purchase things privately is one of my biggest selling points. Not that I am buying things that should be secret—I just like having some privacy from peering eyes on the Internet who will use my purchases against me in the form of advertising.

I also like the fact that cryptocurrency will enable micropayments. I see many opportunities for licensing and copyrights.

I also like that cryptocurrency seems a lot like gold. It has a place in your investment portfolio and that's a great thing.

Now, let me start with what I don't like about crypto.

I don't like the learning curve. I don't care who you are—

crypto is not friendly to the uninitiated. I consider myself to be fairly tech-savvy, and I still have a hard time wrapping my head around some of the concepts. I don't think this can work for the average consumer without a facelift.

I don't like the fact that crypto security is so unstable. The fact that crypto can be stolen on an exchange or the fact that if you lose your wallet seed phrases, you lose all of your money forever is way too scary. Sure, this is true to a certain extent with cash, but crypto just seems scarier, especially when you consider that cyber burglars are way savvier at this than you will ever be. My biggest concern with cash is getting punched in the face at an ATM. The thought of waking up one morning with all your money stolen is a heavy burden.

And if that's not true and I'm wrong, then crypto has a perception problem.

That leads me to the final problem—decentralization. I actually like the decentralization concept, but the problem is the execution. If everything is decentralized and unregulated, that means no one will help you. You're completely on your own, and if something happens to you, it's your fault and there's no way to get justice. I don't like that.

Imagine a completely decentralized world and you can see where I am going with this. I'm not crazy about our current corporate overlords, but at least there's *some* oversight and regulation.

That's why, as I'll discuss later in this book, I believe that investing in cybersecurity will be important for writers in the future.

There has been a lot of talk about smart contracts and how they have the power to disintermediate industries. I believe this to a certain extent, but if you study smart contracts, you'll realize that they're not actual contracts. They're code.

A smart contract will execute no matter what, and when it

does, a third party could find a vulnerability in the code and use it to exploit the contract.

In the real world, that would never happen with a traditional contract because third parties don't know about the existence of a contract. Therefore, if smart contracts take off, we'll live in a future where contracts will have to be defended after deployment, which will require a mixture of a lawyer and a programmer, a profession that doesn't quite exist yet.

And again, when you factor in decentralization, you're on your own and you have to trust that you're dealing with an honest actor when you hire out a smart contract, which puts you back at square one as far as contracts go.

Those are just some of the thoughts I've had about cryptocurrency over the last few weeks. I still don't think we have seen the technology evolve into what it will ultimately be yet, and that's exciting.

In many ways, it reminds me of the early 2000s Internet. It's so foreign a concept that we can't yet see how it will impact society. I don't think anyone would have realized in 2003 the impact that the Internet would have on just the next decade, let alone human civilization.

DECENTRALIZED SOCIAL MEDIA

While researching cryptocurrencies, I stumbled across a service called Bitclout, which is one of the first decentralized social media platforms (known as DESO).

Social media platforms today are centralized. This means that one company (or in the case of Facebook, one person) controls the rules, what you see, and what you can and cannot say.

The social media apps of the future will be decentralized. This means that the community will decide what is and isn't acceptable, and if you don't like it, you can find another community that acts in accordance with your values. There will be many, many decentralized social media apps.

Bitclout aims to be the first of these decentralized social media platforms, and it has interesting ideas.

The platform was originally founded by a mysterious person, which is always suspect to me. However, that person eventually revealed their identity.

Bitclout is similar to Twitter in that it has a newsfeed and it encourages short but thoughtful posts from creators. However, the major difference is that every creator has their own "coin." If

I signed up, I would have a "Michael La Ronn" coin, which is its own cryptocurrency. As I build more clout on the platform, more people can buy my coin. The more follows, likes, and shares I receive, the more my coin grows in value. If I do something stupid (like committing sexual harassment), or piss people off in the community, my coin value goes down.

In many ways, Bitclout is Twitter meets the stock market, where your reputation is your currency. That's incredibly profound.

If users like my content, they can send me micropayments of $0.04, $4, $40, or $400, so my content is technically monetized. That is also profound. Today on Twitter, nobody sends me any money when I make a killer post...

Honestly, when I first discovered Bitclout, I was beyond impressed with the idea. It's probably one of the best ideas for a social media platform I've ever heard.

There are problems, though.

The biggest problem is that the "coins" can't be redeemed for anything. So even if I have a "Michael La Ronn" coin, I can't cash it out. The same goes for any micropayments sent to me on the platform.

Another problem is that the company committed a ballsy marketing tactic that I think was in poor taste. They imported the top 15,000 Twitter profiles onto the platform and gave them their own coins, which sounds great, but they didn't tell the users about it! At the time of this writing, Elon Musk has the most expensive coin on the platform, and he's not a user.

If the company was really serious about recruiting influencers, why couldn't they have approached, say, the top 100 Twitter users over six months, got them on board, and then used them as a marketing tool? The entire scheme just smells funny to me.

Finally, there are many allegations that the service is a scam.

I won't go into the reasons, but I do think the criticisms are valid.

Will Bitclout amount to anything? I don't know. But it demonstrates a proof of concept that I believe *will* catch hold in the near future—creator reputations linked to cryptocurrency.

Bitclout won't be the last decentralized social media platform. Someone is going to take the lessons learned and apply them to a new platform, and then we'll see this platform hit the mainstream.

People are disillusioned with social media companies right now, and many are looking for ways to give them the middle finger. If a decentralized social media platform came along that offered similar functionality to existing apps (which is what attracted people in the first place) but with greater privacy, no newsfeed or algorithms that manipulate you, and ethical development that isn't designed to maximize your time on the platform, while also giving people free speech, freedom, and the ability to create communities around shared beliefs, I think people will be extremely receptive to it, especially if they can monetize their social interactions. This is a solution that people don't know they want yet.

That said, these services could also fan the flames of racism, xenophobia, and all the wrong values in our society, but that's one of the prices you pay for decentralization. If you support it, you have to support the beautiful and the ugly. But I believe the days of everyone being on the same social media platform and consuming the same content in their newsfeed are dead no matter how you slice it.

LOOKING FORWARD

IF I WERE STARTING AGAIN TODAY

I thought it would be fun to start the inaugural "Looking Forward" section by looking back.

If I were starting my publishing business over today, what would I do differently knowing what I know now?

It's such an interesting question. 2014 was much different from 2022.

In 2014:

- Self-publishing was just maturing.
- There was a lot of information for authors, but not all of it was as helpful as it is today. Today, you can find answers to almost every problem you have.
- There weren't nearly as many distributors and book retailers as there are today.
- Audiobooks as we know them were in their infancy.
- We didn't have nearly as many publishing tools as we have today.

The biggest difference is the amount of knowledge you can find.

If I were to start my career today, here's how I would do it.

First, I would write my first book as quickly as possible without letting myself get stuck in cycles of self-doubt. My goal would be to get it published as quickly as possible. If I had taken half the time it took me to write my first novel, I would have published my first book in the middle of 2013, and maybe I would have been able to see some of the original "Kindle gold rush."

That first book is critical, and I'd write it as quickly as possible, ship it to a copyeditor and a proofreader, and call it good.

I would invest in learning how to do my own covers. This would ensure that my early covers would be bad, but I would be okay with that because I know that it's going to take a while to build an audience anyway.

Learning to create my own covers would help me save costs and avoid being tied to the whims of cover designer prices, which I discussed earlier.

I would take the money I could have spent on covers and buy a block of 1000 ISBNs. Yes, you read that correctly. Like I said, I wouldn't waste money this time around.

I would finish my first book (which would be a series), and then I would write the next two books in the series. I would publish them all at the same time, and I would publish them in e-book, paperback, hardcover, and large print. It would be too early for audio. I would publish the books in KDP Select for the first year to maximize my income.

Once the first three books were published, I would run some Amazon Ads on the first book to see how it performs with readers. Then, I would book some other little promos here and there to see what happens. This would be mainly to learn the ins and outs of pay-per-click advertising, not to goose sales.

But most importantly, I would be writing my next books. I wouldn't jump into marketing with any real force until I had at least ten books, preferably in the same series and genre. This would maximize my marketing dollars.

I would invest my money in writing craft workshops.

I would build an author website and also build a mailing list, using the back of my books to do so.

I would invest in technology like Book Funnel to deliver direct sales to my readers.

I suppose this chapter is saying that I would do most everything the same except for my big mistakes. I would use technology and data to their full extent, as a lot of tools weren't available when I started. I wouldn't have been so afraid of Microsoft Excel in the early years either.

I am writing this chapter because I *know* that the answer to this question will be radically different in ten years. I'm very curious what my answer will be then!

OVERWHELMED AND DISORGANIZED: HOW I CLIMBED OUT OF A RUT

In the third quarter of 2021, I found myself disorganized. I had just finished my annual Beast Mode challenge, and for the first time in five years, I didn't have to worry about law school classes.

It should have been a time for celebration, yet I felt overwhelmed.

My email inbox was cascading with emails, some that hadn't been replied to in weeks. I had so many emails that I had no idea who was emailing me. I stayed on top of fan-mail, but I had let everything else go. Just thinking about my email gave me anxiety.

I made several errors in publishing some of my Beast Mode books, and those errors were now manifesting themselves. Things like publishing at the wrong price, misplacing files, rushed book descriptions, and more. It was hurting my income.

My tax situation was a disaster. I had gotten negligent in cataloging my expenses and income.

And, to top it all off, my personal affairs weren't in great shape either.

I hit rock bottom one day. I decided that I had to fix this problem not now, but once and for all.

I am a productive person. I get more done before breakfast than some people do in an entire day. I am programmed to think in systems. But sometimes systems break. What happened was that Beast Mode broke my systems. I knew this was going to happen to a certain extent because it happened last year too, but this year was worse. Fortunately, this is a once-a-year problem, but I realized that there were many areas in my writing business where I could have been more organized, to begin with.

If I were to start my career today, knowing what I know now, how would I organize my writing operations?

I made a list of everything in my writing business and committed to organizing it logically. This took several months.

Here are some of the items I cleaned up.

Cloud storage services. My folders had gotten a little messy over the years, so I spent an afternoon organizing folders and deleting files and folders that I no longer needed.

My book files. Did I have all the necessary files for each of my books, like covers, source files, contracts with designers, and so on? I spent several weeks combing through my book files to determine whether I had everything. After that experience, I wrote a book called *Keep Your Books Selling,* which captured my lessons learned. It taught me a lot about what it means to be organized. I found a lot of gaps. For example, for one of my books, I forgot to secure a license for a font on the cover. I bought it, but I didn't save it. I had to hunt it down. It was a lot of little stuff like that, but all the little stuff added up. By the end of the experience, I was supremely organized. The time I spent doing this will keep me up-to-date for at least the next decade.

My sales pages. I reviewed my books on all retailers and corrected errors in pricing, book descriptions, keywords, categories, and so on. This was a lot of work. I also developed a system to track all of my books.

My computer hard drive. I deleted applications that I was no longer using. I also updated all existing apps on my machine to improve performance. I also invested in software that helped me clean up my computer and improve its performance.

My external hard drives. They needed some cleaning up and maintenance too.

My online account passwords. I had become lax in my passwords over the last few years. It was time to update them, record passwords that I didn't track, and do some general account maintenance. I also invested in a new password manager that helped me keep everything organized. I also took this opportunity to enable two-factor authentication on as many accounts as possible. I learned how to use an authenticator app, and I purchased a few hardware security keys. Now my accounts are as secure as possible.

My tax documents. I gathered all of my expenses for the year and organized them. I came up with a better system for tracking my expenses. I finally broke down and started using QuickBooks.

My notes. I keep a digital notebook in Evernote of ideas that I come up with. I have many, many notes. But I don't like Evernote, so I migrated my notes to Bear. In the process, I cleaned up my notebooks and organized them a little more logically so I can find things better.

My Kindle collections. My e-book collection was a mess, so I cleaned that up and cataloged my books.

My website. I swept my websites and cleaned up broken links, typos, and outdated content.

Email addresses. I cleaned up my email folders and

simplified my emails. I also deleted mountains of emails that I no longer needed, reducing my email storage footprint.

My safe deposit box. I have a lot of stuff in my safe deposit box, so I took a trip to the bank and reviewed the contents.

My storage room. I have a room in my basement with a bunch of books and old stuff. I took a weekend and sorted through it, giving things away, listing things on Facebook for locals to buy, and throwing some things in the garbage. I have fewer things now, and that's a beautiful thing!

Existing work. I have a dozen or so short stories that have been sitting on my computer for years. They're finished and should be published in a collection, but I haven't gotten around to it yet. Shame on me. I plan to address this in 2022.

Those are just a few of the items I cleaned up and organized. Then, I climbed out of my existing rut. It was important to me to clean everything up first before addressing my current problem. This ensured that once I cleaned up and got everything up-to-date, that I would stay up-to-date for a long time. I started this project in the third quarter of 2021 but didn't finish it until the first quarter of 2022.

Running a publishing business is a lot of work. You don't always get it right in the beginning. You can always go back and fix mistakes. You can always clean up your act!

THE COSTS OF COVER DESIGN
CONTINUE TO RISE

The costs of cover design continue to rise. The beginning of a new year is always the time you'll see rates increase, so I benchmarked a few designers who I've been following closely to see where they are at the beginning of 2022.

- Designer A raised their rates from $350 to $450, which is a 28 percent increase.
- Designer B raised their rates from $400 to $750, which is an 87 percent increase.
- Designer C raised their rates from $300 to $600, which is a 100 percent increase.

The costs keep rising, and I'm shocked that more authors aren't raising hell about it. I've only heard one major podcast mention it, and that was in passing.

Why are designers raising rates?

First, the common reason is that they are receiving more work and need to price their time accordingly. They may also need to hire virtual assistants to help them. They may also be paying increased prices for storage devices, technology to create their artwork, and art supplies. Those are acceptable and understandable reasons.

But are they the only reasons?

What about the pandemic? What if a spouse was laid off or sick?

What about inflation and the fact that everything costs more? What about where the designer lives? Wouldn't it stand to reason that a designer in rural Iowa would potentially charge less than a designer in Malibu because their overhead is less?

I don't know the answer, and I am not saying designers shouldn't raise their rates. I *am* saying that this type of year-over-year change is unsustainable, and it will dampen many indie authors' output, or worse, put them out of business. There's no regulation on what designers should charge, and the amount they charge is specific to each designer's situation.

In the designers I benchmarked, the average cost of a cover increased from $350 to $600, which is an average increase of 72 percent year-over-year. In 2025, the cost of these three cover designers will be over $2000 on average. Even if I'm too high in my estimate, the average cost will almost certainly be over $1000. If you think I'm exaggerating, write me in three years.

In the meantime, I'll be designing my own covers. I'll be writing about this in Q2.

LESSONS IN LICENSING: WHERE IN THE WORLD IS CARMEN SANDIEGO?

Recently, I was feeling nostalgic and searched for the *Where in the World is Carmen Sandiego* franchise. I had many fond memories of playing the computer games, reading the books, and watching the game show in the nineties.

When I was writing *The Author Heir Handbook*, I used the franchise as an excellent example of how copyright licensing works. However, I decided that it would be better to use a book example so I used the *Harry Potter* series instead.

I kept the text that I originally wrote and decided to put it here because I learned a lot about how the series has been licensed over the years.

The *Where in the World is Carmen Sandiego* franchise started as a computer game in the late eighties. It was about a globetrotting, cunning supervillain. It merged geographic education with detective novel elements. The series was created to cultivate and inspire children to take an interest in geography.

The *Carmen Sandiego* series began as a series of hit

computer games—*Where in the World is Carmen Sandiego?*, *Where in Time is Carmen Sandiego?*, and *Where in the USA is Carmen Sandiego?*, just to name a few.

Then, in the nineties, something happened that would completely change the franchise forever—the creators turned the idea into a hit game show for kids in the United States and Canada. Every kid in the nineties wanted to be a contestant on that show. The sales of the video games and other associated products exploded.

Anyone who remembers the game show remembers the catchy acapella theme song too—the creators also created a soundtrack for the show that they sold on CDs.

The franchise expanded to include console video games, many series of novels, merchandise, activity books for children, and most recently, a television show on Netflix.

All of this because of one idea: the original video game.

Just to reiterate, what could have been just one video game became many different intellectual properties.

And here's where the magic of copyright lies: the creators of the franchise didn't sell their copyrights. They "licensed" them. When you sell something, it becomes the property of another person or company. When you license it, you only license part of the copyright to someone else, and you keep the rest. So, when the creators of Carmen Sandiego licensed the television show, they kept the rights to everything else. This is how they were able to capitalize on the brand, spinning off product after product. They licensed the game show to two public television stations, a series of novels to a major publisher, a television show to Netflix, and so on. But at the end of the day, the creators never sold the franchise. All of the products they licensed became streams of income that flowed back to the company, which allowed them to create even more products.

That's the beauty of copyright when done properly: you

license it, not sell it. If you remember that copyright is an infinite bundle of rights, then anything is possible!

ESTATE PLANNING CONSULTATIONS WITH ATTORNEYS

In researching *The Author Estate Handbook*, I consulted with several different estate planning attorneys to talk about my family and author situation. Two of the consultations in particular were worth sharing. One was with an estate planning attorney; the other was with an estate planning attorney who specialized in copyright and author estates.

Both attorneys and I had good conversations about steps I can take now to preserve the legacy of my books and how to keep them in a position of earning income for my family after I'm gone. Most importantly, the attorneys gave me advice on how to avoid leaving a mess.

This chapter is a loose, cleaned-up summary of my notes. Do with this information what you will. None of this is legal advice, but merely info to get you thinking about this.

When you die, an estate is opened in your name to transfer your assets.

When you die, your executor has to create a reporting inventory that contains a list of all your assets and their value. That includes any books or copyrights you may own. How do you value your copyrights? No one really knows for sure, and every situation is different.

In many states, the reporting inventory is public record (which is a little scary if you think about it). Do you want everyone in the world knowing what your books are worth after you die? What if one of your books hits it really big and attracts a film studio? Do you want them to know how a court valued the book as they're preparing to make your family an offer?

You must value your inventory so that you can value the estate. Valuation is also for taxes. When you die, the government is entitled to a portion of your estate.

If you're not careful, if your book IP is worth more than your estate, then your heirs will have to file for bankruptcy.

The value you place on your IP is completely different from what a court will. Courts don't care about your feelings, and they won't buy an author's excuse that a book isn't worth much. It's worth whatever they say it's worth. And your heirs may not like the end result.

There are a few different taxes the government can assess.

In the United States, there are estate taxes (also known as death taxes). At the federal level, this tax applies to multimillionaire estates. At the state level, the thresholds are lower.

There are also estate income taxes, which are taxes on income generated by your estate after you die.

And finally, there is an inheritance tax, which is paid by your heirs upon receiving your estate.

You won't have to pay all the taxes I listed above. In some states, you will pay no tax on your estate after death. In some states, you will pay an inheritance tax but not an estate tax. It depends on where you live.

Every attorney will recommend a will, a power of attorney, and if applicable, a trust.

Wills are common knowledge and I won't explain them here. Trusts are worth discussing, however.

The main reason to set up a trust is that, by doing so, your reporting inventory is no longer public record. Therefore, you maintain some privacy. Also, you can transfer your copyrights into a trust and have your family (trustees) manage them (more on this later). This also applies to your book income. This way, you can control how, who, what, when, where and so on when it comes to the money. You can also ensure that your heirs won't sell your copyrights on a whim because they need to pay rent (known as squandering). However, setting up a trust incorrectly and not following legal guidelines can be just as bad as dying without a will and making your family go through probate.

On average, an attorney will take on average two percent of the value of the estate, so it pays to keep the value of your estate down!

Quotes I received from a few different attorneys to do wills and a trust was about $500 for a will and $1500 for wills and a trust. Not cheap by any means, but it can save your family in probate costs, which are very, very expensive and can easily land in the thousands, minimum.

Here's what I learned from the copyright attorney.

What are the pros and cons of putting your copyrights into a will versus a trust versus a publishing corporation you own?

If you leave your copyrights to someone via a will, the copyrights will go through probate, thus creating many of the problems I mentioned above.

If you leave your copyrights to a trust while you're alive, you'll avoid probate, but there's the problem of copyright termination. Under copyright termination (in the United States), you can revert your rights after 35 years. It's designed to protect authors from bad contracts they sign early in their careers. The termination right also passes to your heirs after death. If you have dishonest heirs, they can invoke copyright termination, pull your copyrights out of the trust, and then squander them. They cannot do this if you leave copyrights through a will. You can leave your copyrights to a trust via your will through what's called a pour-over provision. This may help to prevent the copyrights from going through probate.

If you leave your copyrights to your publishing corporation while you're alive, the same issues remain with copyright termination.

Leaving your copyrights to a trust or a company also has tax considerations. Trusts have some of the highest tax rates in the United States. It may be more favorable tax-wise to leave your copyrights to your publishing company, but it depends on your situation.

I can't guarantee that any of the information above will be helpful for your situation, but it's a reminder that there's a big world out there. You may be focused on just finishing your first book, and that's the smartest thing to do. The writing life is hard enough without having to think about all this stuff, trust me— and I know that better than anyone.

But at some point, you have to pull your head out of your manuscript and learn the business side of things. If you don't, you could be damaging the legacy you want to leave as an author.

ESTATE PLANNING LESSONS

Estate planning was a focus for me this quarter. I wanted to document some more lessons I learned while writing *The Author Estate Handbook*.

Estate planning just isn't discussed in the indie community. It's not sexy and it doesn't create income. But if you don't plan for what will happen to your books after you die, your books will die with you.

To make the problem worse, there's a lack of information on estate planning for writers. You can find many resources on estate planning for regular people, but sometimes that advice is bad for authors.

In reviewing my will, I discovered the unpleasant reality of this. My attorney really screwed me in my will, and I had no idea until I did my research. I document how in *The Author Estate Handbook*, but if I had relied on this attorney's advice, I would have wrecked my estate.

I learned that there are so many pitfalls with wills for writers. Unless you get some help from a copyright attorney, a traditional estate attorney can really mess your will up. This is because they don't always understand copyright. Yet, I suspect that most authors will rely on what their attorney tells them without question. Read my section on wills in the book and you will see how scary this can be.

I learned about the power of trusts and how amazing they can be as estate planning tools. I promptly set up a revocable living trust for my family.

I learned just how critical usernames and passwords are. Sure, I knew this before, but my research showed me first-hand scenarios about how deadly not leaving passwords can be. Your heirs won't have a fighting chance.

I also learned about two-factor authentication and how dangerous it is as well. I don't know if many people are using two-factor authentication properly. If they died tomorrow, I am convinced that most heirs would not have access to the author's codes. I talk about why in the book. My learnings in two-factor authentication were perhaps the most eye-opening in my research. It scared the crap out of me, because if your heirs can't get your two-factor passcodes, they can't get into your account, even if they have your username and password. Read that last sentence again.

I learned a lot about banks and how they treat accounts when a customer dies. That was also eye-opening and scary. I realized I wasn't taking the proper steps to ensure that my family has access to my business funds after my death. I quickly corrected that.

I also learned about how retailers and distributors treat your publishing accounts when you die. This is a tricky, complicated topic. The short answer is the terms of service control what happens. Some retailers require your heir to create a new account and republish your titles. Others allow the heir to keep the existing account, but they must take several steps to get the account changed. If they don't have the username and password, they're SOL.

My research also took me down paths I didn't expect, like how my heirs will be targets for scams, how to treat posthumous work, or how I want my estate to communicate with my readers after my death.

The Author Estate Handbook is perhaps the most detailed nonfiction book I have written. I cover a lot of ground and spend a lot of time in minutia, but I hope it will be as helpful for writers as it was for me to write it.

If you'd like to check out the book, you can buy it at www. authorlevelup.com/estatehandbook.

WEB 3.0 TRENDS

It's time for me to create a new website in the next few years. I keep saying that I am going to do it, but then I don't because I realize that web technology is evolving and I want to make sure that the next version of my website is built on a stable footing.

Besides, any changes I make to the website at this point would be cosmetic and technical. It's not an urgent need.

I've been researching Web 3.0 to see where the future of the internet is going. If I can figure out what author websites will look like in ten years, I can start designing my vision of what it will look like now.

In a previous volume of this series, I outlined the features that my new website needs to have:

- better design
- more sales-driven functionality to get the right book to the right reader at the right time
- up-to-date with all the latest web standards and best practices
- Web 3.0 ready, even if that functionality is not needed at the moment

Some of the research I've been finding on Web 3.0 is...interesting, to say the least. I think Web 3.0 is weird, and I say that as someone who came of age around the advent of Web 2.0.

I used to work for a web development company that specialized in bringing businesses from Web 1.0 to Web 2.0.

Web 1.0 was the original Internet, with flat, poorly designed web pages. It was known as the "read-only" Internet.

Web 2.0 connected people to each other and facilitated the interaction between websites. Social media, search engines as we know them today, application programming interfaces (APIs)—that's all Web 2.0. I was drafting Web 2.0 proposals for businesses as early as 2008.

Now we are moving into Web 3.0, which is built on artificial intelligence and the blockchain. Web 3.0 is about connecting the Internet of Things (IoT), artificial intelligence, blockchain, machine learning, virtual and augmented reality, cryptocurrencies, and other emerging technology to each other. Whereas Web 2.0 was about connecting people, Web 3.0 is about connecting things so that it makes our lives less labor-intensive.

That's just the beginning. I don't think we truly know what Web 3.0 will bring. Here were some of the things I found in my research that indicate what could be coming.

The Semantic Web. Current web technology uses keywords and categories to determine what content is. Search engines can't "read" or analyze content effectively. The semantic web will use machine learning and artificial intelligence to analyze content and make recommendations to users based on what they are looking for at the time. While companies like Google and Amazon can do this today to a limited extent, in the future, all websites will be connected. You won't receive just the benefit of Google's expertise—everyone will leverage each other's knowledge through machine learning to create hyper-accurate results, and it will be decentralized. It's intriguing to think that the walled gardens we have today (Amazon, Google, and so on) will be broken down.

I see a few opportunities for authors in this technology. First, if keywords and categories are eliminated, it's possible that books could breed their own metadata. Many in the industry have been advocating for this for years. Wouldn't it be nice if a retailer could scan your book and recommend it to people based on the actual content of the books? This would eliminate the rampant category abuse on places like Amazon, and it would revolutionize the BISAC system that the book industry uses for categorizing books.

I also see this as a cure for the discoverability problem. When someone searches for a certain genre, they'll get hyper-accurate recommendations based on their history, preferences, and dislikes. Therefore, search engines and retailers can start recommending books that historically have been on the long tail to readers. Books that were making coffee money could suddenly become popular because the content will matter. This could radically shift the balance of power and bring books into the fray that have been there all along but ignored. This is one of the reasons why I keep saying that the authors with the biggest backlists will win.

Three-dimensional websites. I played around with a few 3D websites and they were weird. But imagine a website where the content exists on a plane where you can navigate it with a character or avatar. One website I explored was a map of a 17th-century French town. You could click around and explore it. It reminded me of a gimmicky Flash website from the early 2000s, but much slicker. This technology could make it easier for authors to create interactive experiences with their books. I'm still convinced this part of Web 3.0 is a gimmick. It's the first thing people talk about. I believe it will be more than this.

Users owning and monetizing their data. Today, when you use Facebook, you don't get paid for it. Tomorrow, when you use the social media apps of the future, you will. People can send you money in cryptocurrencies, and if the company uses your data to create a product or service, it will automatically send money to your wallet.

The metaverse. You will be able to use virtual and augmented reality to visit virtual locations and connect with people in person instead of by text on a website, such as a comment. Take a site like YouTube. When you watch a video and want to comment, you interact with other users by typing comments. In the future, you might log in to the metaverse, watch the video in a virtual room, and then chat with other avatars who were also watching the video. Or, you might be able to hear conversations about a video a la Clubhouse and *watch* people get into arguments rather than read them. Now, imagine people doing this on a book review page. Every book's review section could become a book club (or a fight club). This could take the concept of "building a community around a book" to a completely new level.

Decentralization. People are getting fed up with big tech companies abusing their data and manipulating them. Many people are going to support decentralized apps (dApps) which will perform many of the same functions as big tech apps, but without the data and privacy issues. What if there was a decentralized book retailer who used the semantic web as a way for readers to find books? And what if this retailer allowed authors to publish books on it? It could be a mixture of Amazon and Goodreads, with authors being compensated every time someone purchases a book. It could even facilitate micropayments, with the author getting paid by pages read. Everyone who uses the app receives a share in how the website is run, meaning that the website serves as a co-op of sorts. Will it be as sophisticated as Amazon? Absolutely not, but it would be an interesting mashup of Amazon, Kindle Unlimited, Goodreads, blockchain, cryptocurrencies, and an e-reading app.

I'm just getting started, and I'm still exploring Web 3.0, but those were the features that stood out to me. Based on my initial research, I believe the following action items are clear:

- Think of your author website as an experience, not a website.
- Spend less time focusing on categories and keywords and cataloging your content in the future and more time understanding what content looks and feels like in a given genre. Today, we focus on copying the style of other authors as a way to signal to readers what our books are about. We need to start focusing on what authors are doing within the pages of their books, which will require deeper concentration and more research. Eventually, tools will be able to help us with this.
- The future belongs to authors who specialize in genres. The further down you can niche your writing and understand competitive books, the more you will be able to write works that will be recommended by future Web 3.0 algorithms.
- Accepting and paying in cryptocurrencies is a must. While the technology doesn't quite exist yet and there are many, many cryptocurrencies, the websites of the future will need some way to accept crypto from users (and even pay users in crypto). This will need to be right next to your standard retailer links.
- Beware of fads. There will be a lot of them as Web 3.0 gets started.

- Application programming interfaces will continue to be important with Web 3.0 because they will connect websites and services to each other. I predict that APIs will become easier to use and more websites will use them.
- Understanding cybersecurity in a Web 3.0 world will be more important than ever, and you can start that today.

I'm excited to see where Web 3.0 takes us, though I'm not necessarily looking forward to the time and energy it will take to develop a new website for it.

CYBERSECURITY FOR AUTHORS IS THE FUTURE

In 2020, I created a course called *Writing in Hard Times*. I recorded it during the COVID-19 lockdown and released it for free to the community at the time. The course is about identifying threats to your writing business, developing contingency plans, and learning about future threats.

When I put the course for sale, it promptly died. Only one person has purchased it. I believe it is one of the most important pieces of content in my catalog. In it, I talked about cybersecurity and how it is a growing threat for authors.

When most people think of cybersecurity risk, they think of big companies getting hacked. It seems like every week there is a news article about a company suffering a cyberattack or a ransom attack.

However, if you look at the statistics, the most common targets for cyberattacks are small businesses. One of the growing sectors of targeted businesses is contractors, and if you think about it, it makes a lot of sense. Many contractors don't necessarily have technological sophistication. That's not a knock on contractors. They are easy targets.

Authors are small businesses too. It's just a matter of time before someone realizes we're easy targets.

Think about it. Do authors use cybersecurity best practices to protect their data? Probably not, because they don't think they are targets.

If you were hit with a cyberattack tomorrow, what would you do? What would you do if a hacker locked your computer and demanded $1000 in Bitcoin? Would you pay it? Who would you even call to get tech help?

What if your reader's information was stolen, like credit card information or email addresses? Would you be required to report it to the government?

These are important questions that we as a community are unprepared for.

You can purchase cyber insurance for this type of exposure. It used to be relatively cheap, but the cost is increasing because cyberattacks have been rampant since the COVID-19 pandemic.

In this volume, I've spent a lot of time talking about emerging technology like cryptocurrencies, blockchain, and decentralization. Soon, cybersecurity is going to become even more important and your most valuable data is going to be at even more risk than it is today.

Therefore, cybersecurity needs to be a focus for writers of the future.

What does that look like? I'm not sure yet. But I think authors need to be extremely careful. We're heading into uncharted waters as far as security goes, and it's hard to know what types of technology and tools will exist to help us protect our identities, currency, and data. This is an area of concern for me and something I will be paying more attention to in the coming years.

SOME THOUGHTS ON THE PACE OF TECHNOLOGY

As I documented my opinions and lessons learned in this quarter's volume, I realized that this volume has perhaps the widest range of topics of the entire series.

There are chapters on writing craft, productivity, large print editions, publishing data and analytics, book distribution, artificial intelligence, blockchain applications, cryptocurrencies, Web 3.0, ISBNs, copyright licensing, automation, estate planning, and more!

Wow, what a dizzying list!

This range of topics is remarkable for a few reasons.

I've found myself unable to focus on just one technology lately. It's not because I have difficulty focusing—it's because so much technology is dependent on each other. I don't see that changing in the future. I believe it will make sense to think holistically about the writing business because everything will matter.

I am also getting the sense that we're on the cusp of another technological wave that will completely change the way we do business. I've said this over the last three years, but I especially believe it will be true within the next five years.

In this section alone, I've discussed several factors that I believe will change the author profession. In the next section, I'll discuss more.

I missed the last wave that transformed the author business (self-publishing). I was too young to capitalize on the early days of self-publishing from 2009 to 2013. I joined in 2014, and I've always felt I was late to the party (which couldn't be further from the truth, but I still feel like it).

I've always promised myself that I won't miss the next wave, but the next wave isn't going to look anything like the one that hit in 2009.

I predict that the next wave is going to put a lot of authors out of business. It's going to take them by surprise, and the technological advancement is going to leave a lot of people behind.

In the early days of the self-publishing revolution, the pioneers were the authors who:

- dared to publish their work without a publisher
- were traditionally-published but reverted the rights to their work so they could self-publish it

People mocked self-published authors. It was still a stigma back then. (It still is now, but it's more commonly accepted).

The people who especially mocked indie authors were those who romanticized the old way of doing business—traditional publishing. Many of those authors either came to their senses or were left behind, their careers strangled by draconian publishing contracts and hefty doses of self-doubt and self-sabotage.

As I look at the next ten years, I see a convergence of many technologies:

- the reduction of the importance of smartphones and devices
- cryptocurrencies and blockchain technologies such as smart contracts
- Web 3.0
- virtual reality, augmented reality, and the metaverse
- rapid decentralization across many sectors
- artificial intelligence, machine learning, and automation
- and more

Navigating each of these will require skill sets that we do not have yet.

Also, many of these technologies are not as immediately intuitive as tech in the early 2000s and early 2010s.

For example, I can explain the technology behind an EPUB to even the least tech-savvy of writers, and they will get it. Even if they don't, they can use a simple application to help them achieve industry-standard e-books.

As a counterpoint, I *cannot* yet explain the blockchain to someone without them looking at me sideways. And if someone wanted to use a blockchain application, they would have no idea where to start. Whether you're initiated or not, it's complicated.

And that's the problem. The average self-published author today is used to preparing e-books and paperbacks, uploading them to retailers, and using tools like Book Funnel or Payhip as an added technology layer. While we claim to be a technology-driven industry, we are not. Almost everything we do is manual, though we do benefit from some automation.

Will people still want to read books in the future? Will the concept of a book change?

What happens if reader preferences do change? Will indie authors adapt? Really, though—will they? Or will they do exactly what many did at the beginning of the self-publishing revolution, which is romanticize the way they do business?

Given the impending future that is on the way (and in some respects, here now), it'd be awfully easy to want to protect the status quo of publishing. There's something simple and quaint about writing books, uploading them, doing some marketing, and enjoying the benefit of your hard work. Why mess around with blockchains, AI, Web 3.0, and other technology that has a deep learning curve and requires a skill set that many authors currently do not have?

That's what I think will happen. It's human nature. Therefore, I must resist that nature and try to see the potential in any new technology despite criticisms, however valid those criticisms are.

I believe 2022 is the last full year to get my fundamentals in order. Change is coming, and I want to be ready when it arrives so I can take advantage of it...repeatedly. When December 31st, 2022 arrives, I will stand ready to finally become the writer of the future—the result of several years of planning.

What are the fundamentals?

- Sound business fundamentals and a good tax strategy.
- Being a writing machine, writing more books than the average author per year with less effort.
- Creating manuscripts with fewer errors than the average author's.
- Turning the art of publishing into a science by creating high-quality, well-packaged books on day one.
- Maximized distribution, meaning the books are available to buy everywhere humanly possible.

- Maximized formats, meaning the books are available in as many formats as I can manage.
- A reliable and sizable community of people willing to buy my books on day one.
- A good, up-to-date website that gets the right book to the right reader at the right time.
- The ability to track expenses using automation.
- The ability to track book sales using automation.
- The ability to use data to make informed decisions about the business.
- Reducing costs wherever possible to keep the business lean and ready for anything. This means learning to do your own covers.
- Supreme organization skills.
- An estate plan that takes care of your family.
- Chaining all of these elements together with technology to increase my efficiency and deliver more value to my readers.

Those are the fundamentals, and after this year, I'll have put those behind me. I may still need to make some improvements, but all of my fundamentals will be working together harmoniously.

Then, in 2023, I'm going to be entering a new world, developing new skill sets, and venturing down new routes.

It's a little scary to think about, but if I do this now, I'll be in a much better position to capitalize on the next wave of technology that is sure to arrive soon.

If I fail to get my fundamentals in order, as I believe many authors will fail to do, then I won't have the capacity, time, or money to invest in new technology, which means I will get left behind. I don't plan on getting left behind, so this is going to be a fun year!

Q1 2022 PROGRESS REPORT

2022 is a fresh year for me because I've streamlined my goals. It feels good to have fewer targets to aim for.

BECOME A WORLD-CLASS CONTENT CREATOR

To achieve my goal of becoming a world-class content creator, I will focus on the following tactical priorities:

- Demonstrate a commitment to learning the craft of storytelling and teaching
- Demonstrate a commitment to outstanding quality AND quantity

Examples of day-to-day activities that will help me carry out my tactical priorities include:

- Keep learning through online courses and workshops taught by professional writers who are further down the path I want to walk
- Reading
- Developing mentorships
- Finding new ways to increase my daily word counts
- Mastering different writing methods
- Documenting my process of becoming a successful writer in the *Indie Author Confidential* series
- Cleaning up my platform to ensure a consistent quality reader experience

What did I do to become a world-class content creator during Q1 2022?

- I have taken approximately 15 workshops from Dean Wesley Smith and Kristine Kathryn Rusch on writing craft.
- I have read (and studied the craft in) 12 books so far this year.
- I am on track to publish 100 books by the end of 2023.
- I adopted Sudowrite into my writing routine, helping to increase my writing sessions by an average of 200-500 words per session.
- I bought 1000 ISBNs and expanded my potential distribution into bookstores and libraries by publishing with IngramSpark.
- I expanded my distribution into StreetLib, giving me access to new international markets. I'll complete the process of listing all of my books with them by the end of 2022.

- I expanded my day one publication process to include hardcovers and large print editions.
- I have returned to making regular weekly YouTube content.
- I organized all areas of my writing platform to be more productive and efficient in creating new work.

BECOME A TECHNOLOGY AND DATA-DRIVEN WRITER

To achieve my goal of becoming a technology and data-driven writer, I will focus on the following tactical priorities:

- Use technology to make the business more efficient
- Use data to get insights

Examples of day-to-day activities that will help me carry out my tactical priorities include:

- Developing a tax plan
- Developing an estate plan assisted with technology
- Learning how to design my own covers
- Hiring a personal assistant for small tasks where it makes sense
- Developing a metadata database for my work
- Improving my readers' experience on my website
- Implementing direct sales for my fiction

What did I do to become a more technology and data-driven writer during Q1 2022?

- I developed a solid tax strategy for 2022 that will minimize my tax liability, with a longer-term plan for the next three to five years that will further shrink the amount of taxes I owe to the government...legally.
- I created my estate plan to ensure that I will leave a legacy as well as income for my family after I'm gone. This included an updated will, a revocable living trust, and helpful documents my heirs can use to run my publishing business.
- I created a master publishing file for my books that gives me insights into how my books are listed as well as potential opportunities to maximize the portfolio. I am now extremely organized and able to manage my book portfolio with the same skill and ease as someone who only has a few books.
- I've started researching the possibilities of cryptocurrencies and blockchain and how I can utilize them to move into the future.

I'm off to a great start for 2022. Next quarter, my focus will shift to learning the basics of cover design and maximizing the value of my book portfolio.

As I said in a previous chapter, 2022 is the final year for me to get my fundamentals right. I'm excited about that, and I'm looking forward to what the next quarter brings.

CONTENT CREATED WHILE WRITING THIS BOOK

This section recaps the books I've published and media I've created during the quarter. To keep the book evergreen, I will not include links to podcasts or magazine articles because sometimes links break over time, especially with podcasts if the hosts stop podcasting. You can easily search for them to see if they're still active at the time you're reading this book. If they are, enjoy! If not, please accept my apologies.

Books

Keep Your Books Selling

M.L. Ronn covers the process he followed to organize his book portfolio and make more money. If you've ever wanted to get more organized and know what's going on with your books across all retailers, this book will help. It will help you keep your books selling.

Buy at www.authorlevelup.com/selling.

· · ·

The Author Estate Handbook

This book will help you plan for what will eventually happen to your books after you die. Organize your affairs and leave a legacy that you will be proud of. More importantly, leave a portfolio of books that mints money for your heirs long after you're gone.

Buy at www.authorlevelup.com/estatehandbook.

The Author Heir Handbook

The book for overwhelmed heirs who need help managing an author estate. The perfect book to buy for your heirs while you're still alive. This concise book is written in plain English with many examples to help them understand publishing, business, and marketing.

Buy at www.authorlevelup.com/heirhandbook.

Magazine Articles

"How Law School Made Me a More Business-Savvy Writer." *Writer's Digest*, January/February 2022 Edition.

In this article, Michael shares his major learnings from law school and how he applied them to his writing business.

Podcast/Video Appearances

"Interview with Michael La Ronn" on the Ken and G Podcast.

In this interview, Michael talks about beating writer's block and how to be more productive.

.   .   .

"Masayuki Uemura Tribute" on the Ken and G Podcast.

In this interview, which is a complete 180 from what he normally does, Michael discusses his top 5 Super Nintendo games.

"Interview with Michael La Ronn" at Valley of Writers.

In this interview, Michael shares productivity tips and his process for writing quickly and efficiently.

"Writing App Speed-Dating." *Writer's Digest* Virtual Novel Writing Conference 2022 (available to purchase).

In this talk, Michael discusses the hottest new writing apps and the technologies powering them. You'll learn major trends in writing apps and features you didn't know existed. You might even find a new perfect match!

READ THE NEXT VOLUME

Michael's writer journey continues in the next volume of this series!

Grab your copy at www.authorlevelup.com/confidential.

MEET M.L. RONN

Science fiction and fantasy on the wild side!

M.L. Ronn (Michael La Ronn) is the author of many science fiction and fantasy novels including *The Good Necromancer*, *Android X*, and *The Last Dragon Lord* series.

In 2012, a life-threatening illness made him realize that storytelling was his #1 passion. He's devoted his life to writing ever since, making up whatever story makes him fall out of his chair laughing the hardest. Every day.

Learn more about Michael
www.authorlevelup.com (for writers)
www.michaellaronn.com (fiction)

MORE BOOKS BY M.L. RONN

Books for Writers:

www.authorlevelup.com/books

Fiction:
www.michaellaronn.com/books

www.ingramcontent.com/pod-product-compliance
Lightning Source LLC
Chambersburg PA
CBHW022100020426
42335CB00012B/761